W9-CZU-297

SALLE

ELIZABETH AVEDON EDITIONS

VINTAGE CONTEMPORARY ARTISTS

VINTAGE BOOKS

A DIVISION OF RANDOM HOUSE NEW YORK

A Vintage Contemporary Artists Original, November 1987
FIRST EDITION

Copyright © 1987 by Elizabeth Avedon

Library of Congress Cataloging-in-Publication Data
Salle, David, 1952–
David Salle.
(Vintage contemporary artists)
"Elizabeth Avedon editions."
"A Vintage original"—T.p. verso.
Bibliography: p. 85
1. Salle, David, 1952–   —Interviews.
2. Artists—United States—Interviews.
3. Art, American.   4. Art,
Modern—20th century—United States.
I. Schjeldahl, Peter.   II. Title.   III. Series.
N6537.S28A35   1987   709'.2'4   87-40466
ISBN 0-394-74788-7 (pbk.)

COVER PHOTOGRAPH © 1987 BY RICHARD AVEDON

BACK COVER: The Loneliness of Clothes, 1986.
Oil, light bulbs/canvas; 108″ x 90″. Collection of
Eli and Edye Broad, Los Angeles. Courtesy
Mary Boone Gallery. Photo: Zindman/Fremont.

Manufactured in the United States of America
10   9   8   7   6   5   4   3   2   1

AN INTERVIEW

WITH

DAVID SALLE

BY PETER SCHJELDAHL

INTRODUCTION

"That's David Salle," an acquaintance said at an opening in 1980, indicating the dark-featured chap whose intensity, an electric tension between eagerness and wariness, had drawn my notice. A bit wary myself, I immediately contrived to meet him. In that year of art-world upheaval, when a sudden phalanx of young painters and photographic artists was changing the face of the culture, Salle's usually mispronounced name ("Sally" is correct) was much in the air. Fascination and suspicion, even fear, attended rumors of his enigmatic work, underground prestige and commercial success. Though less well known than his friend Julian Schnabel, whose scandalous self-assertion had an infectiously open, generous aspect, the astringent Salle was even more disturbing to art-world veterans. I had seen a few of his pictures, with their bluntly drawn erotic and melodramatic images on fields of acrid color, and had been at first jarred then baffled, then increasingly stirred by them. They were like ready-made dreams, as intimate as if I had dreamed them myself, and utterly fresh.

My first reaction on meeting this twenty-seven-year-old phenom was, I'm afraid, a trifle smug. Simply, he was so transparently, wildly ambitious—even by the standards of his generation, whose common style of impatient self-assurance I had begun to recognize—that I almost laughed at him. Instead I complimented him (why not be magnanimous?) by telling him my interpretation of one of his paintings. His face registered pleasant surprise and something else, flickering in his gaze: serious, thoughtful, total

3

disagreement. I was glimpsing a formidably intelligent point of view, as disconcerting as a rock in a snowball. I have been disconcerted—amused, awed—by David Salle ever since.

That initial encounter changed my life as an art critic, not that it happened right away. I found that the more I studied Salle's work, the more I grasped the generality of new art then exploding in the U.S., Germany and Italy. He seemed to cover wholly things that other interesting artists had this or that piece of: pictorial irony, imagery-as-nature, aesthetic skepticism, eroticism and theatricality, the elements of a wised-up contemporary baroque. He also had his share of certain new tones, of harshness and brashness, that I found troubling. But a glance at his art could dissolve all my reservations in astonishment; and the established art world's response to Salle, akin to that of white corpuscles greeting a disease germ, polarized me in his favor. My conviction of his significance hardened in the face of reflexive and often vicious attacks from every conceivable quarter.

Salle's career no longer resembles that of a rising politician or boxer, a series of public events that teeter between triumph and disaster. His standing as a major artist, like him or not, is secure, and the focus of current artistic controversy has moved elsewhere. But he continues to represent, for me, the primary case and test of art-for-art's-sake in the eighties. He continues to claim aesthetic license in dealing with all manner of meaning and material. That, beyond the sheer visual and poetic sophistication that his work demands of viewers, is probably what most upsets people in this era of politically tendentious criticism, when art is judged less by experience than by loyalty oath. His stubborn use of pornography-like female images is only one of his provocations, though the most contested. He is scarcely alone among contemporary artists in pushing permissible boundaries, but he is the one most purely committed to aggrandizing the aesthetic—the pleasure principle at its most ramified, refined and ruthless—over every other consideration.

David Salle was brought up in a culture-conscious Jewish family in Wichita, Kansas. He was already an abstract painter before attending the seminal California Institute of the Arts in the early seventies. There he switched from painting to conceptual and installation work. In many ways the most revealing and certainly the least known part of his story is that of roughly the years 1974 to 1979, when he found his way in the foggy regions of a downtown New York art scene far different from the spangled arena it is today. That was a fecund time for Salle and his entire generation —young artists fed up with the lingering orthodoxies of the sixties, fiercely skeptical of prevailing values and determined to mount, somehow, a tough response to image-glutted contemporary reality. The first mature work of this generation coincided with a dramatic upswing in the art market, causing a public impression of styles and careers given virgin birth by fashion. "Downtown in the Seventies," the first of this interview's five parts, should help correct that simplistic notion.

"Painting Again," the second part, explores the personal and aesthetic process of Salle's return to painting in the middle seventies. "Dance and Autonomy" jumps over the intervening years of his career, which seem sufficiently a matter of public record to be scanted here, to his present preoccupation with stage design, notably for dances choreographed by Karole Armitage. His working relationship with Armitage is one of the really remarkable collaborations of recent times, and his remarks on it are, for me, the heart of this interview. It has plainly brought about not only an extension, but also a deepening and clarification of his enterprise. Salle also vents his considerable spleen on the subject of critics, as all artists are wont to do; but he does it with animation and bite beyond the ordinary, and with good cause. The lack of engaged critical mediation in our culture is an ongoing crisis particularly for art, like Salle's, that is actually or implicitly theatrical, hence dependent on a responsive audience. Another kind of crisis comes for artists in mid-career, when so many (most, even) seem to lose their way as if to prove F. Scott Fitzgerald's thesis that there are no second acts in American lives. Salle worries aloud about it in "Keeping Going." Finally we just talk painting, with an emphasis on the erotic mysteries of that archaic but persistent art.

FOOLING WITH YOUR HAIR, 1985.
Oil/canvas; 88½″ × 180¼″ (4).
Collection of the artist. Courtesy Mary Boone Gallery.
Photo: Zindman/Fremont.

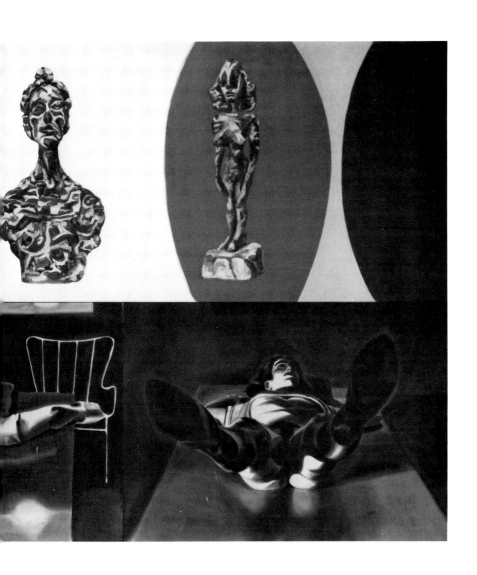

I

DOWNTOWN IN THE
SEVENTIES

PS: When did you come to New York?

DS: I came, I don't know, sometime during 1974, to seriously as opposed to touristically look around at where artists lived and how they lived, to see if it was something I thought I could do. And then I finally did come, more or less for good, in the late summer of 1975, and had arranged a very cheap sublet apartment on the corner of Broome and Varick. It happened to be next door to where Claes Oldenburg lived. But I never saw him.

PS: Who did you know in New York then?

DS: There had been at Cal Arts a couple of people who had already made that leap. I'm talking about California, but I think it probably was true whether you went to school in California or Wisconsin or even sometimes as near as Boston; the way one lived without going to New York was in a kind of speculative holding pattern, a dreamy sort of way, telling yourself that you were doing this either because New York was finished and you didn't need to go there, or because you wanted to go there on your own terms, or you wanted to go there when you felt like you had a body of work, et cetera. Whatever you told yourself, what one did if one didn't go to New York was basically just do different forms of worrying about why one wasn't going to New York. And there were a number of people who had already stopped worrying about it and had just gone.

PS: Who?

DS: Ross Bleckner, who had grown up in New York, and who had some family support behind him, was set up in what at that time seemed like the unattainable goal, his own loft with separate quarters for living and painting, and furniture and a real refrigerator and things like that. And at that time Ross was a little bit like the Godfather insofar as he had this loft, he knew people, he could dispense favors.

PS: *Who were members of the mob, then?*

DS: (laughter) Well, the other people who had also come earlier included Matt Mullican, who had a relatively easy adaptation to New York not because he had any money, but because he had very bohemian parents and was accustomed to living a very improvised and self-contained existence wherever he was. Matt lived on Twelfth Street and University Place in a little apartment that was actually half of someone else's apartment, and it was divided with a blanket tacked on a wooden frame to make a wall, but of course when the person on the other side of the blanket was home, it was just like living with someone in the same apartment. Matt Mullican, in his own primitive bohemian way, and Ross, in his official artist's way, were already set up in New York when I arrived. There were other people here that I knew, most of whom were friends of Ross's, painters whose work started to be noticed in the late sixties, and by the mid-seventies, the time I met them, were experiencing all the different kinds of aesthetic crises that one can experience.

PS: *It was a time of disaster for painters. There was almost no critical support, no market, no agreed principles; it was still a time when minimalist sculpture and thinking dominated. . . .*

DS: Well, I think that many of these painters—I wasn't very close to them, but I did know them—had virtually stopped working. This is something that no one would ever come out and say, but I remember many people who had really, although they had studios and called themselves painters and held academic posts in painting, stopped working. I remember paintings staying in people's studios—when they said they were working on them—for months and months, not much happening. More than anything else that was happening in the galleries or the magazines, that was really indicative of what was and was not going on. It was funny to be young oneself, and to be in contact with people who had lost their reason to work.

PS: *You yourself had stopped painting at Cal Arts. And moved into conceptual work.*

DS: I had been painting in my own way since I was a kid and felt as though I was very committed to painting, but in fact I stopped almost immediately as soon as something more utopian and less frustrating came along. I just gave it up flat. Which amuses me to think about it now, how easily I walked away from it.

PS: *What did seem possible then?*

DS: What I think now is not what I may actually have thought then, but this is what I remember. It didn't really matter so much what form work took. Work could take the form of something that happened in real time, like a performance, or something that happened in some combination of theatrical and real time, like a film or videotape, or work could be an object on the wall, a drawing or painting or photograph or a series of photographs or even a text. I don't think that I had a particular feeling for the form something had or ought to take. But I felt a dissatisfaction with what seemed like the available forms.

PS: *It seems to have been a moment almost without viable role models. Who came closest to being one?*

DS: Well, when I think of that time, it seems to me that everybody was simply trying to find a way to say to the world that he was an artist. That's what was really going on. And the question of what kind of artist, an artist to what end, why an artist—those questions simply couldn't be answered at that time, because all of the energy went into simply trying to say that one *was* an artist. So much doubt surrounded the practice of art in the first place, and so much doubt surrounded any particular form that it might take and all transactions within all the forms—transactions between the artist and the audience, the artist and the system that distributed the work or exhibited the work—that there simply wasn't enough psychic room for people to consider what kind of art they were making and what kinds of things they wanted to say. People who seemed to be most successful at establishing some kind of viability for their even being artists in the first place were the ones who had a charismatic attraction and effect on other artists. There were some people who may not have been known outside of very small circles. I remember a performance artist named Julia Hayward. This was the time when people took new names, which is something I've never understood very well. Anyway, Julia Hayward went by the name of Duca Delight. She made performances which combined her talents for storytelling and manipulation of language, combining an anecdotal sense of storytelling with this feeling for rhyme and coincidence and synonym in a way that was very interesting and made one think in a primitivistic way about James Joyce, and yet also was musical and a little bit racy, which was fun. People like Julia Hayward, whom you've probably never even heard of, were by far the most charismatic.

PS: Where would you encounter her work?

DS: Well, we would go to the Kitchen and pay two dollars and sit on the floor. In my generation there were, I would say, more people working in that kind of relationship to the art audience than there were people making exhibitions of paintings. What the interesting people wanted to say in their work, or the feeling they wanted to have, needed the most fluid kind of form. Performance art, which is a degrading name, was, in some people's hands, just exhibitionism. But it could be the barely-held-together form that could contain and not overrun these fragile feelings of images and word pictures connecting and disconnecting like an alternating current.

PS: My reminiscence of those times is that the world of contemporary art seemed like little tribes gathered in dark corners while the world rushed by outside and took no notice whatsoever. Did you do performances?

DS: I didn't, not after I left art school. I did make two installations, both at the Kitchen, which had their requisite fifty-person audience. These situations were not reviewed, typically, so no record was made of them. They were ephemeral, which, like all art, enhanced their poignancy somewhat. I'm still trying to answer the question of who else seemed to be providing a window to the "something else." . . .

PS: Remember people like Vito Acconci or—

DS: Oh, Vito! That's funny, I had completely forgotten about him. Vito was a vortexlike figure for many, many young artists. And Vito did do gallery installations at that time, and they were well attended and much discussed.

PS: The major one was when he masturbated under a ramp.

DS: Well, the famous masturbation installation was before my time in New York; that was in '72 or '73. I met Vito in California and when I came to New York spent some time with him, wrote a brief essay about his work, talked with him a fair amount, worked in his studio on a couple of projects, and appeared briefly in his magnum opus videotape, *The Red Tapes,* which was shown at the Whitney Museum and was widely considered to be a masterpiece, the pinnacle of performance-video-linguistic-postpainterly art. I wonder how it would look now. I remember it as having the right doses of imagistic invention and audacious cultural longing and posing. Of course Vito's primary device was the winning salaciousness of his

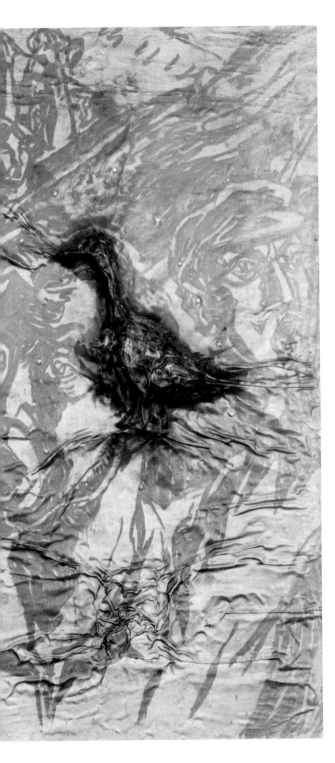

PAUPER, 1984.
Acrylic, lead/canvas;
84″ × 106″ (2).
Collection of Jane
and Robert Meyerhoff,
Phoenix, Maryland.
Photo: Zindman/Fremont.

honesty, his "confessions," which created a terrifically *present* feeling for the audience.

PS: *What did you do in the tape?*

DS: My appearance in the tape is very brief. It occurs at the end. Erika Beckmann and someone else and myself run around in a space, only seen from the shoulders down, and we have some dialogue; I can't remember it. I had by far the smallest part. Erika had a significant part.

PS: *Were people like Robert Longo and Cindy Sherman, from Buffalo, on the scene yet?*

DS: The Buffalo crowd came down to New York quite a bit later.

PS: *What were you doing for a living, by the way?*

DS: The first thing I did when I came to New York was to teach drawing two or three days a week in a small college in New Jersey. After that dried up, I supported myself for a while by working in people's studios, Vito being one of them, and by cooking in restaurants. Mickey Ruskin had opened a new restaurant, The Lower Manhattan Ocean Club, and Julian [Schnabel] was to be the chef. I had met Julian through Ross, and he talked Mickey into hiring me as a cook. And that's what we did for a while.

PS: *What was the conversation like, with Julian, in those days?*

DS: I remember very little talk about art with Julian. I remember much more about living situations, not having a place to paint, being treated like a dog. I mean, the drama of the degradation of daily life was much more the kind of constant theme. There was also a good bit of humor about it all.

PS: *What kind of reception were you getting from the art establishment* in New York, your generation, the galleries, the museum people, the critics?

DS: Well, I was getting absolutely no reception whatsoever. What little public exposure I had was in very small, alternative-space-type galleries—sometimes in Holland, sometimes in New York, places like the Kitchen. The Kitchen wasn't on the Listings sheet in *The New Yorker* yet. I remember when Robert Longo came to New York and got the job as the administrator of the Kitchen, we used to go every Friday night to see whatever was there, because we could get in free. There was no waiting list then or a public relations person and all the things that followed very shortly after. I remember going to the Kitchen once to see Jonathan Richmond and the Modern Lovers, whom I was very interested in at the time. I went with the Cal Arts crowd, Matt and Erika, Susan Davis and a couple of other people, and we were the only people in the audience. There was simply no one else interested.

PS: *So meanwhile you were going around to museums and galleries, I presume, and getting a sense of what was being recognized.*

DS: Mmm-hmmm.

PS: *How did it look to you?*

DS: I can't remember much that we saw in those days, really.

PS: *Well, you mentioned showing in Holland. One peculiarity of your generation was that it arrived on a scene in New York that had been insulated from much awareness of Europe, and you were aware that things were going on there.*

DS: Well, this is one of the things that Cal Arts had been very strong in fostering; I don't know how deliberate it was. The primary person that we had contact with at Cal Arts was John Baldessari. This is all very well documented in lots of places. John's

17

own career had never really amounted to very much in New York but had been quite active in Europe, very active at certain times, really. He was considered something of an underground hero in Europe.

PS: *Europe embraced late minimalism and conceptualism, people like Bruce Nauman, for instance, to a degree that the United States didn't.*

DS: Right. Now, at school, we were not even connected to the Southern California art scene; we were completely in our own world at Cal Arts. We were not aware that everyone in the world didn't have the same information that we had, or didn't consider things in a way at least similar to the way we considered them. When I moved to California—you and I have talked about this many times—in 1970, the primary person that I wanted to meet was Bruce Nauman, whose work was like a compass point for me at that time and continued to be for many years afterward. I thought Bruce was one of the most important artists in the world. And I sought him out, which is something that I never did with anybody else; I was never that brazen to just call someone up out of the blue and invite myself over to their studio just to see what their studio looked like. I mean, we just simply didn't have any idea that Bruce wasn't as highly thought of in New York and that his retrospective at the Whitney sort of flopped and that few people collected his work and that Leo [Castelli] lost money on him. We simply had no idea that this was the case. We considered Bruce to be a celebrity of enormous magnitude.

PS: *I think one of the interesting stories of your generation—of any generation, but one that is as significant as yours—is how its originality is maybe the last thing it discovers, the last thing that becomes self-conscious.*

DS: This may have to do with John's influence as a teacher. John did little teaching in any normal sense of the word, but what John did was to make everything that occurred in the art world so normal, so much a function of the way things are, that we really didn't have any idea that this level of information wasn't shared by everyone. John was, quite simply, interested in every single thing that happened in the name of art almost equally. He didn't really differentiate between forms. He had a personal taste, he preferred some things over other things, but the point to his presence as a teacher was that it was a big world, there was room for lots of things, everything was potentially interesting. And on the other hand, the corollary message was that nothing was all that great either. Art was just what people did.

PS: *That was part of, from my point of view at the time, the terrible grayness of the seventies. Everything mattered to a degree, but nothing mattered very much and it was just an immense swamp. But then, of course, I wasn't aware of you or the very large number of people who were swimming around in it.*

DS: Well, in retrospect, I think it was probably a good atmosphere to have grown up in, although at that time I think it created a feeling of dismalness. Through John, we were very much aware of nothing being that impressive except the very rare, very special isolated cases. What was interesting is that like all situations where disciples magnify the attitudes of gurus, I think John was probably horrified when he realized that what it resulted in was that we simply weren't impressed by anything, period. Part of that is just being in art school. But I think it was very good armor when coming to New York, that idea of not seeing anything as more than someone's trying to do something more or less interesting. I remember this was also a time of big international group shows. When people talk about big international group shows now, they mean something like "Zeitgeist" [Berlin, 1982], but then the international group show meant something like the opening of P.S. 1 where it was international to the extent that some Italian artists, Anselmo or some others, or Richard Long—whatever the roster was—would be given a space and a budget for materials, usually very low, and just be told to do something in that space, to install

19

something, make something, alter the space in some way, or not alter the space as they chose. That was the kind of big international group show, New York group show, that was in vogue when I was in art school, and when I came to New York, the model for it being probably Documenta. It wasn't a show, it was just a roll call.

PS: *Very rarely would there be any painting in them.*

DS: There was almost never a painting. People painted on walls. But our cynicism had become so deep and so pervasive, I remember seeing John at the opening of P.S. 1 and complaining that everything was shit, and why were they making such a big deal out of this. You know, because there was a lavish party, and people were clearly trying to pretend they had pulled off something kind of wonderful, kind of terribly important. We were bitterly disappointed. I remember John looking at me like I wasn't supposed to take it that far, saying something like, "Look, kid. This is as good as it gets, so stop complaining." But, of course, I really think it was his cynicism that had sort of unleashed our cynicism. But our cynicism went much deeper; it was much more real than his ever could have been. And of course it affected the course our work would take.

PS: *What were you living for?*

DS: Well, that's a good question. Sheer contrariness.

PS: *What were you reading? Was anything you were reading affecting you?*

DS: I wasn't reading a great deal. The one author I can recall being very involved with was Peter Handke, whose work I had encountered when I was in California. The first book of his that I found was the book of poems the title of which had been translated as *The Inner World of the Outer World of the Inner World.* I haven't reread it since 1975 or 1976 or so, but I remember feeling that the tone of the work rhymed rather perfectly with the kind of feeling I had about life at the time. The aesthetic ambition was appropriately very high at the same time as the feeling of the work was rather bleak—bleak isn't quite the right word. Lots of things can be bleak without being interesting. There was a sense of the writing coming out of a very stripped-down, fundamental position using words in a deliberate, aesthetic way to create this *thing* that seemed to me to be very interesting. And apart from reading Handke's works as they appeared in English over the next few years, I think I was primarily affected by the work of certain film directors, primarily Douglas Sirk, and to a lesser degree Sam Fuller and then some of the Germans. At that time Fassbinder and Herzog movies were starting to be shown in New York. Another director whose work I discovered upon arriving in New York and who remained an example of the submerging of an absurdist vision in an overall structure was Preston Sturges. And there was something very up-to-the-minute and fine-edged about his movies, even though they had been made quite early, even before Sirk.

PS: A *pure, denatured hysteria?*

DS: Sturges was the surreal comedian, but Sirk was the first hyper-real artist. You see . . . I thought of Douglas Sirk as a very great tragedian. I remember seeing *Imitation of Life* at the Museum of Modern Art with Sherrie Levine. We used to go to movies together. I remember saying to her afterward that I really despaired of ever being able to make anything this great, a work of art anywhere near as great as that film. I saw that film many times subsequently, and that feeling never went away. I haven't seen it for several years. I don't know if now it would look to me like it does to most people.

The main thing about Sirk's movies that was very compelling was how strange—something that is easy to overlook—they look, how incredibly beautiful the visual component is. What that implies is a sense of deliberateness to make a visual world—a very strict visual world that is composed of certain very clearly premeditated elements. There is almost always a sense of very deep space or broad space in a Sirk frame. His cameraman, Russell Metty, was one of the great cinematographers of that era—the late forties and early fifties—and Sirk was one of the first people, with Metty, to use color in this way that still for me carries a great deal of meaning. The films are almost always shot in a very high key in terms of light and color. And there is deep space and strong use of verticals in the composition of the picture; these give a sense of the sugary surface of the reality of American life, and the structure of the drama, the text, is the underside of that same world. The way that he was able to make one manifest through the other I thought was quite brilliant and really unparalleled. It is the opposite of the kind of naturalism—or the so-called naturalism—that has overtaken Hollywood cinema in the past fifteen years. There is also even on the visual level a sense of the European absurdist in Sirk's movies. There is an extreme edge to the costuming, lighting, coloration of the set—the use of artifice that I am sure by viewers at the time was not noticed and was not intended to be noticed. It struck me as exemplary—an exemplary degree of self-consciousness and control—visual control on the part of the artist in calling your attention to how he felt about the subject matter without there being any apparent intrusion of interpretive morality into the context. There are also a number of black-and-white films, and perhaps in the black-and-white films the extent to which Sirk was visually poetic is even more apparent in the use of light and shadow and composition to give meaning to certain elements of the drama of the text. I think these are the kinds of things that are very important in my work and are similarly not noticed, or at least are not recognized or felt, by most of those people who have taken it upon themselves to comment about the work. That is to say that what I would consider the artfulness of things in some cases is really invisible, or it becomes visible in a particular and unusually slow way.

PS: *I don't suppose you were yet aware of Fassbinder in Germany?*

DS: Yes, we were very aware of Fassbinder.

PS: *You were? Because he was a great devotee of Sirk.*

DS: We had heard of Fassbinder when I was in California. I don't think there had been any screenings of his films yet. But certainly in '75, '76, '77, I spent those years looking at Sirk, Fassbinder, Fuller, and Preston Sturges. I think those directors more than anything that was happening in the galleries were what gave me something to make art for, something to strive for aesthetically.

COLOR PLATES

BYRON'S REFERENCE TO WELLINGTON, 1987.
Acrylic, oil/canvas; 102″ × 103″ (3).
Private collection, New York.
Courtesy Mary Boone Gallery.
Photo: Zindman/Fremont.

MINER, 1985. Oil, wood and metal, tables/fabric, canvas; 96″ × 162½″ (2).
Collection of Philip Johnson, New Canaan, Connecticut.
Courtesy Mary Boone Gallery. Photo: Zindman/Fremont.

GÉRICAULT'S ARM, 1985.
Oil/canvas; 78″ × 96″ (2).
Collection of Museum of Modern Art, New York.
Courtesy Mary Boone Gallery.
Photo: Zindman/Fremont.

I I

PAINTING AGAIN

PS: When did you start painting again?

DS: I started in the practical sense in the winter of 1976. I had made works for a show at Artists Space that Helen Weiner arranged for me to have. In that show there were works on very large pieces of seamless backdrop paper. In each of these works there were three or four different kinds of images brought together on the surface of large pieces of paper, large rectangles.

PS: What were the images?

DS: Well, I just have to go piece by piece and describe; I don't want to list them in terms of categories. In one painting there was an image of a tree, a sequence of drawn images of a tree growing, combined with circles. Another work was the image of splashed paint, a woman holding her breasts, and the word *Camus*.

After that exhibition, and after growing tired of carting around these large rolls of paper, I had an impulse, felt an impulse to literally shrink; I'm not sure exactly why. Partly because I was quite broke and socially withdrawn, but whatever the impulse, whatever the origin of the impulse, after this show in 1976 the works I made were much smaller. I began making the prints as a way of creating an image without having to be involved in painting it but still being able to have a picture or an image. What I resorted to was something in the nature of a silhouette, which I'd never realized before this moment is something that continues to figure in the work up to this time. This is a very roundabout answer to when and how I started painting again after the years of conceptual

31

dabbling: I began making the block prints, no bigger than two or three inches across, that depicted things, scenes. For example, the most satisfying one was a tiny silhouette of a man and a woman seemingly having an argument, standing next to each other, with the man making a gesture with his arms, and the woman, I believe, making an imploring gesture. And next to them was presumably the same man lying on the ground with a pool of blood around his head, as if there were two frames, before and after, although the after image was oddly on the left side. Several things interested me about this, this image, not the least of which was how much the narrative and emotional information could be contained in this tiny silhouette. And how interesting it was, the effect of putting something that should have been on one side, on the other side. The space, the mental space opened up by that was something that has always interested me. And it was in line, *more* than in line with my ongoing propensity to see things in a slightly altered form next to the original, in reference—things in repetition but not exact repetition. I applied the block print images to unprimed canvas more or less all over. I stretched the canvas because I wasn't really interested in making any kind of statement about the materials. And produced, in this very unpainterly way, that is to say without using a brush or really painting anything at all, the first painting that I made in several years. This is very early in 1976. I made a number of these works, using block prints and oftentimes marking on top of them with charcoal. Looking back on it now, the paintings were materially so sketchy, but they were satisfying to me as paintings.

PS: *There was an extremely defensive and hostile posture toward the world among artists then. Part of it was political, the aftermath of Vietnam, and there was a bias against the market, not that there was any market with the big economic recession in the seventies.*

DS: Yes, of course, but at that time I wasn't aware of it. I wasn't aware that these events were taking place against the virtual collapse of the market. I wasn't aware of a market for paintings or works or art to begin with. And if I had been aware of it, it wouldn't have meant anything because I had no experience of it.

PS: *Were you getting a confirming response from the people around you?*

DS: Not particularly. There was always a handful of people who assumed that what I was doing was interesting without really looking at it too carefully. And the people who weren't already interested, I don't think gave it a second thought.

PS: *Meanwhile, you went to Europe.*

DS: Well, I had contact with Europe in letters. As I said, there was an alternative space in Holland, the director of which was a friend who was interested in my work and had presented some pieces in his space in group shows. I think the first time I went to Europe as an artist was either in 1977 or 1978. I can't remember exactly. But the role of European art in this narrative has gotten all distorted. There is a formulaic assumption about Americans in the seventies going to Europe to pick up clues in the aftermath of modernism's demise in New York. Needless to say, that is something of an oversimplification.

PS: *You went with Eric Fischl?*

DS: Well, I had gone to Europe before going with Eric. There was one trip in particular that was somewhat eventful during which I met up with Eric—who at that time was living in Canada—in Germany. We traveled in Germany together and we saw a number of interesting things, one of which was the exhibition of Jörg Immendorff's *Café Deutschland* paintings, which was a lucky thing to have seen. It was at the Michael Werner Gallery. It is somewhat interesting how all of this has ended up being knitted together.[1] But again I wouldn't want to overstress any of these things as *influences.* The other thing I remember seeing in Germany during that summer's trip that was very powerful was a show of Nauman's at Conrad Fisher's in Düsseldorf. So I think the point is to try to see what was actually happening at that time rather than deciding that one group or another group held the right cards. It was more a matter of some constellation of individuals, each one working in more or less different styles or materials or means, having more or less success coming up with something that felt significant or real.

PS: You had shared a studio with Eric at Cal Arts?

DS: The first year I was in school, our class had a very large, barnlike building, and in that studio Eric and I worked in the same room. We were very close. After graduating I hadn't seen him for quite a while. I'd lost touch with him more or less; he was living in Halifax.

PS: I'll point out that Eric arrived in New York by a much more roundabout route. He didn't really settle until the late seventies.

DS: Halifax had a much closer connection to Europe than any-place else in North America. When I was in Germany with Eric, he knew about some things that I had only heard of, like Immen-dorff and A. R. Penck and Sigmar Polke, for example. I had heard of them, but I don't think I had ever seen anything. We went to the Basel Kunstmuseum, which had an enormous drawing retro-spective of Penck, who at that time still lived in the East; he hadn't yet escaped. I thought the work was very lively and I ad-mired its obsessive self-referentiality. I admired it; I thought Penck's work was kind of sexy in a way. It had a kind of libidinous Eastern European quality that I associate with some Czech and Polish cinema. These are societies that are virtually unaffected by things like feminism, or rather where the relationships between men and women are so much determined by the state that certain kinds of ribaldry and eroticism are just like a big slow river. I don't know why it is, but it's different. I liked that, and I was impressed by the sheer volume of the output. I knew Illeana Sonnabend a little, through John Baldessari. I was curious to know what she thought about Penck. I remember seeing her on the steps of the museum, and she was shaking her head sadly, and I said, "Well, what do you think?" She said, "Not very original, I'm afraid." That was as recently as 1978 or 1977; I can't remember which. I don't know what point that makes, except that it illustrates how quickly things can change when there's a reason for them to change.[2]

PS: *The European figures who might be thought of as having any common wavelength with your work would be Polke and Gerhard Richter.*

DS: Richter's work I knew quite well through friends in Holland who had worked with him. I hadn't seen much in person, but I'd seen a lot in reproduction. Sigmar's work was the same; I knew it primarily through reproduction, and I'd seen very little. I knew it less well.

PS: *Well, he had been working with a stylistic device which you have used to great effect, the overlay. Can you remember the first time you put one image over another?*

DS: The advent of the stylistic device of the overlay really has nothing to do with either Polke or Picabia. At the time I did it, I was ignorant of Picabia, except for the early mechanistic paintings. I painted the image of a woman smoking a cigarette on top of a field of other images so that I could see them *through* her—look through her to them. I remember doing it impulsively, without any premeditation, just knowing that I wanted to see both images at once.

PS: *Well, I can point out that overlay was a very common design trope of the twenties and thirties.*

DS: I wasn't really even aware of it. The Picabias that interested me, which I saw for the first time at Westkunst—I think it was in '80 or '81—were the forties' kitsch ones. In that particular exhibition there were two paintings, *Women with Bulldog* and *Woman with Greek Sculpture*. I was astonished by these paintings; I had simply no idea that paintings like that had been made in the twentieth century. They were so perverse. I was very interested in works where you had trouble figuring out what the intention of the artist was—what it was that he was actually showing you, and what you had to make up to account for it.

PS: Can't imagine anyone in his right mind wanting to do that.

DS: I was struck by the nudes because they have that quality which is similar to the quality that appears in Sirk films of there being a lot under the surface, and of not really knowing the morality of the situation that you're involved in when you look at it—the degree of awareness on the part of the artist.

PS: We're getting into technical matters now, and the device of the overlay, and the way of reifying images, which also has a parallel in Polke's work.

DS: I had been making for three years paintings of a single color with images drawn in charcoal on top of the color, sort of spread around the rectangle of the painting, and they held my attention for several years, but after a while they just seemed to be too mute, mute in not a particularly interesting way. I didn't know what I was going to do. I didn't have an idea of where to push the work.

PS: Where were you getting the images at this point?

DS: They were nude women, occasionally a nude male torso, a Buddha, some car crashes, some airplanes, and a telephone, and occasionally a chair, always the same chair. And all of these images were drawn from photographs that I had found in various places. I just kept reshuffling them, over and over again, in different combinations. It's generally assumed that the starting point for my work is some kind of obsession with popular culture, and that all the images I use are taken from various pop-culture sources. The point about this early work is that I deliberately narrowed the vocabulary, the inventory of *things* to shuffle around because one element always does when one begins to make art—it's like limiting your palettes, which I also did, or deciding to use only black. These images were my materials, they were all I needed, *then,* to keep me occupied, to keep my fantasy sailing along. The works were incredibly simple at this point, little haikus instead of the epics of the last few years. The point is simply that this is not about popular culture, or about appropriation.

I'm a foreigner, really, in the realm of popular culture, and I took images because it was easier than making them up, like using ready-made paint in the sixties. Now most of the images originate in my studio, are carefully, or frivolously staged; and, not that it makes any difference qualitatively, because what really interests me is their orchestration, almost none of the images are drawn from popular culture, unless you think of nineteenth-century iron axheads or still-life fish images (two things I'm using in my work now) as popular.

PS: *You had a job for a while with a soft-core porn magazine? Did that have any effect on your work?*

DS: Well, much has been made about this. It's certainly something that I did. I think it's been latched onto as some sort of explanation for my work, which is totally ridiculous. Those kinds of anecdotal explanations are too logical and have nothing to do with my way of working. It's never that simple. It was just someplace that I worked, among the many places that I worked.

PS: *Doing what?*

DS: I did the paste-up, the lowest task in the art department of a magazine publisher. Other people decided how a page was supposed to look, and I executed it. The company was about to fold. The magazines were very cheap. The principal photography was basically taken from stock photos or picture files, and when I left there, I just helped myself, since they were liquidating the whole company. I emptied out cartons of black-and-white photographs, which I carted around with me from studio to studio for a long time. My way of working was very primitive; it was simply to sift through all these pictures, looking for what, I don't know. There was a wide range of subjects, they weren't all nudes, and they weren't really very explicit nudes. They were women in their underwear, for the most part, and had had a lot of airbrushing done on them to make them *less* explicit if anything. But there were also images in the picture files of all kinds of sporting events and packs of wolves on the tundra—you know, all the subjects that these magazines romanticized about. But I actually *used* very few of these images, and for a relatively short time. For some reason they were obsessed with car crashes. I have a hundred photographs of car crashes. Which, I mean, it seems remarkable now, but at the time it never occurred to me that this was similar material to what Warhol had been fascinated with fifteen years earlier. One of the other main fascinations or fantasies of that genre is flying, being a pilot. There were lots of photographs of private airplanes. And then the two genres coming together—airplane crashes. And then, for the real aficionados, airplanes crashing into cars, airplanes causing car crashes.

PS: *But these are all from a magazine. In the context of the magazine, it's about the constellation of a certain kind of male sensibility. . . .*

DS: The publisher also published seemingly the opposite genre or the corollary genre—women's fantasy magazines. In those, the pictures were mostly of women with handsome men in sports cars, and also maternal images of women with babies, women with neat homes occupied by babies, and so on.

PS: *Let's say you were latching onto a line of cultural paradigms.*

DS: I think you have to keep in mind that my real interest, my real art interest through these years, the years we've been discussing, or one of the primary interests anyway, was Sirk. Seeing it in this context, I think this might make a little more sense than the way this emphasis has been written about. I wasn't interested in *magazines*. People seem to want to make a kind of episodic narrative—you know, that I worked for this magazine with these sexist pictures and my work was born at that time. I think again it's more accurate to see what I was going for, aiming for, as having to do with a classical tradition of surface, a classical tradition of paying very strict attention to surface. If you think about how movies look —the surface that Sirk possessed that contributes to your feeling that there's something terrible going on underneath the surface— and if you keep this image in mind and think about the traditions held by the great ironists who similarly dealt with surface in a very detached way, like Johns and Lichtenstein, two obvious examples —I think you can see a similarity in both of those artists' work in the awareness of something underneath revealed by the meticulous surface—you have a little clearer idea that what was motivating me was certainly something very different from what's usually assumed to be an interest or obsession with popular culture. Interest in popular culture in and of itself sounds very elitist. It simply doesn't have very much to do with my art. That's not what would make something interesting or not interesting art. Whether art is or is not involved with popular culture or the world of American culture is not the issue. In all of these works I've been describing —works that interested me at this time, whether of literature, cinema, painting—what connects them together is perhaps difficult to see. Both narratives—movies (i.e., popular culture) and Europe—are really allegorical tales, and quite misleading. I think that my work and my responses to things have always followed along a particularly American classicism but in a detached, ironical way. Irony is something that is often denigrated in art as being not of the highest seriousness, but, I think, in our world, irony is the most rigorous mechanism of natural selection because of its ability to admit complication and progress. That is to say progress of thinking. In that sense, it's not important to make distinctions about what was and what is or is not American as opposed to what is or is not European. Likewise, whether or not something is involved with popular culture. Anyway, what was popular culture a hundred years ago just looks like a funny old style now. That alone doesn't give it meaning.

PS: Well, I think your work, although it has stayed very much within the edge of contemporary art, was involved in opening out on the world of American culture.

DS: I would be hesitant to say what the real themes of my work are. I think that everyone's work has themes, you know, real themes as distinct from formalist, art themes. Without going too much into what those themes might be, there were two ideas which came together in my mind and formed a very powerful, very potent constellation. As we have said, one was the Sirk mode of tragedy, which some people would call melodrama, where characters act out their fate no matter what they think or no matter what they try to do, because that's the way the world is. Things are what they are because of the way people are. The other idea, which casts an even wider net, was the linguistic idea of "the obligatory," that we're only able to say what, in a sense, can be said. We all speak and think and act within what linguists call the obligatory. I would say a real theme of my work has been to get outside of that, or to address the possibility of transcending that, or at least making it so painfully visible that you can think about what the world would be like if that weren't the case, even though ultimately whether it is or is not the case is not even discussible. I think much art that interests me is about getting outside of oneself.

PS: Do you associate that kind of project with any other artist, or writer?

DS: We already talked about directors and Peter Handke. I could add John Ashbery and Dennis Cooper to this list. I certainly feel like I'm in touch with those kinds of feelings when I look at Rauschenberg's early work.

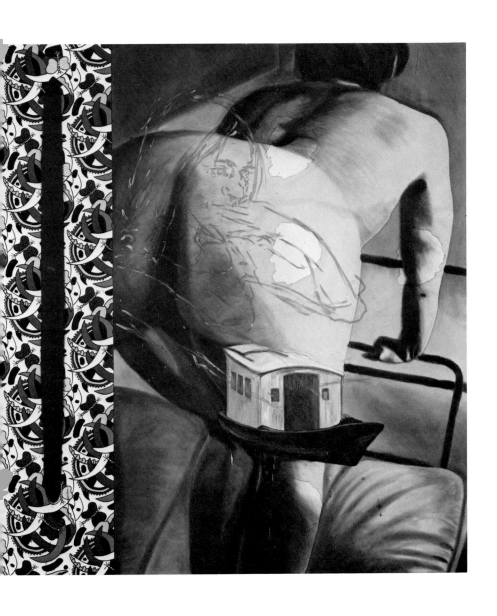

ıs Brain, 1984.
il, acrylic/canvas, fabric; 117″ × 108″.
ollection of Gerald Elliot, Chicago.
ıoto: Zindman/Fremont.

PS: Or Warhol's early work. He seems to have always gloried in the utter predictability of behavior.

DS: I think when Andy's work was great, it was great because of that feeling. But that feeling alone is not enough to make a convincing work of art, and while his later work has that feeling, it's not as interesting. I mean, it has a feeling that's merely depressing. There's a way in which feeling of the obligatory, and this is something that I don't think was ever understood about my work, or about anyone else's for that matter—there's a way it can be incredibly liberating. It's the force of recognition that art can give you. And so, when I say I worked at this magazine, and I got these photographs, I don't think it should be taken as causal. It was just something that happened coincidentally. It was a very apt thing to have happened, and it didn't happen to someone else. But why those images were recognizable as material was because the themes were already there in me.

I I I

DANCE AND AUTONOMY

PS: When did you meet Karole Armitage?

DS: I met Karole backstage after a performance of what was to become a piece called *Paradise*. It was a brief meeting. For years, Karole was in New York infrequently; she was on tour for long periods of time. Whenever I saw her, she was taking a plane the next day and would be away for two or three months. We did finally meet after a work-in-progress performance at the Ukrainian Ballroom.

PS: When was this?

DS: I don't know exactly. It was either '82 or '83. I first saw her perform earlier, probably in 1979, possibly 1980. She was doing a piece titled *Vertige* in which she made an incredibly wild but also extremely precise solo. It was astonishing. I will never forget that feeling of seeing Karole create meaning while dancing, while performing.

PS: This was just in the course of going to performances and dancing?

DS: Friends in Europe had seen Karole perform there. They tipped me off. She was on her way to becoming a kind of cult figure in Europe already. I knew immediately there was something profound and unique going on in this work. This feeling has never left me. I would refer to it in my mind as a touchstone about several things, one of which was about the relationship between work and life. And the other was about the kind of originality I wanted to feel.

PS: *Is there any way you can put into words that new thing you saw?*

DS: It's difficult to describe what's good about dance if it's good. It wasn't simply the fact that Karole's dancing was extreme, which it was, that made it interesting. She is very long-limbed and had amazing extensions and the ability to appear as though all four limbs were working in contradictory ways, but also with complete visual harmony. The fact that it was wild and extreme was simply a condition, one of its conditions. It would have been a mistake to think that what made it interesting was the fact that it was wild. What was interesting about it was that there was something *being made.* She was using new wave rock music and the rhythmical insistence of the dancing took off from and came back to the wall of guitar sound to create an image of a woman who was looking at fate unafraid. This image was not created with acting, which is often the case with dance, but with a controlled *barrage* of steps. This is the point about art that is difficult to get across because it's self-evident to people who see it, and to people who don't see it, it's virtually invisible. Like so many things that interest us in art, or that percolate through art and obsess us, if one has to ask about them, it's unlikely that they will be understood. Not everyone interested in so-called new dance seems to have what Edwin Denby called "susceptibility to dance meaning." If art is any good, it's simply not like everything else. For better or for worse. People who don't see this, who don't perceive this condition, see things which for them become negative. For instance, someone might see pastiche or kitsch or something like that, or they might incorrectly perceive a deliberate technical matter in Karole's case as simply rebellion. People who were not susceptible to it might miss the rhythmical hook. But anyway, that's not really for us to worry about. What I saw in Karole's work was the creation of an entity, a thing that alluded to and resembled other things, stirred your imagination, stirred your linkages to other things but in fact remained a new thing by itself, apart from everything else that it wasn't.

PS: *It seems difficult for people to credit the idea that what they might see, what they see might be what they're supposed to see.*

DS: Yes, and also that what they're seeing is the thing itself. And beyond that, it's a thing that's been made *so that it can be seen.* Sometimes people discuss works of art as if they've happened upon them in a forest, happened upon them in a way which makes you wonder what their images of artists must be. I think that there is a resistance on the part of the audience to acknowledge the degree or level of control that must exist for works of art to be created in the first place. I think it's something that makes people uncomfortable.

PS: Yes, it's difficult to realize that what they're seeing is not a failed something else.

DS: All this is about what I noticed when I realized something was going on. What was happening onstage was something that wasn't a stand-in for something else and didn't point to the feelings you were supposed to be having if you were going to have any. It was those *things;* it wasn't linking arms with something else. It wasn't, in a sense, making way for the footnotes to attach themselves to it. It was exactly what I had wanted to feel but wasn't feeling about works of my generation. And all these things that I'm saying about it, about its not being a stand-in, are exactly to the point of my objection to the level of contemporary art that one saw in New York in the mid-seventies. There is a problem in late modern art which is the problem of metonymy, something being a metonymical figure for something else. I would say it obviously grows out of the utopian desires of modern art, which have to be sort of continually overturned or fought against, and this was something that was not being successfully done in the context of visual art; when I saw Karole dance for the first time, I realized it was something that she was successfully doing. It's like when you know that you're in the presence of a real thing rather than something that is pointing to something else. You're in the presence of something that is a fact in the world and, as such, is unlike any other thing in the world.

PS: So then you met her.

DS: We met after a performance. Part of Karole's costume for that role was red dye on the teeth so that whenever she opened her mouth during a performance you saw a line of red, and from where I was sitting, you couldn't quite believe what you were seeing. You thought maybe it was smeared lipstick or that your eyes were going fuzzy. When I saw her backstage and she opened her mouth to speak, her teeth were in fact red. And the other impression I remember having was that she was, seemed, very tall. That was about it. I didn't see her again until the performance of the complete version of that piece, which was almost two years later.

PS: *When did you get the idea of designing for the stage?*

DS: It came with Karole. I had thought about it in a passing way as something that artists did in the twentieth century. You're aware of that. I don't know if everyone feels this way or not, but you see something interesting and you wonder if you can do it.

PS: *Also the idea of performance and theatricality that's been a keynote of art lately.*

DS: Well, I don't know about lately or not lately, but I think that in my work in particular there are a couple of desires which are, which have been very forceful in pushing the work on and which have a linkage with the theater. One of them is the idea of simultaneity, which of course is connected to the idea of complication, which is one of the reasons for invoking the stoical mask that is irony because of irony's ability to select without selecting. The second idea is a wish to make works that can support an extended viewing time. Now, both of these ideas or desires, simultaneity and prolonged viewing time, are things which happen more easily in the theater than in painting.

PS: *Well, you're very much the director in your paintings. I mean you handle all sorts of elements. But you saw that the entity didn't have to be simple. It could be complex.*

THE ELIZABETHAN PHRASING OF THE LATE ALBERT AYLER,
The Armitage Ballet. Choreography: Karole Armitage. Design: David Salle, 1986.
Dancer: Karole Armitage. Photo: Colette Masson.

DS: Well, I have always had an inability to see something singly. I always see the picture and the wall the picture is on at the same time, almost as the same thing. And I've had to reconcile this with my desire to make autonomous, self-sufficient art. I remember driving down the street in Venice, California, when I was in school and feeling the façades of buildings separating out from the buildings themselves. I saw that everything in this world is simultaneously itself and a representation of the idea of itself. This was in a sense my big art epiphany, and it took a long time for my art to evolve from that starting point—naturally it would be something fairly complex. This was, of course, many years before I had heard any French po-mo [3] simulacrum-type poetics jive. The pleasures and challenges of simultaneity continue to be one of the driving forces in my work. But you also see the thing as more of an abstraction of itself. You see the thing as all of the ideas about it—as a representation. But to take this further, as I've said, I never thought of this stuff that I'm talking about as really counter to formalist autonomy. I mean, what I'm talking about has manifested itself very differently stylistically from what one thinks of as formalist art. But, in my mind, there's no difference between Stella's early work and my own except, of course, perhaps in quality. And I think that the oppositional type of distinction that's made between, say, the aesthetics of minimalism and the aesthetics of my work is for me a false one. I thought that formalist work was about the beauty of the tenuousness of the connection between you and it. And I thought that my work was the logical extension of that. I never thought that I was giving up the formal autonomy of art. I never thought of it as anything other than an extension of New York School paintings. I do remember as a student reading something Stella said that was always reassuring in this department, which was that he wanted to be able to paint like Velásquez. He really wanted to paint paintings like Velásquez, but since that was out of the question he painted stripes instead. As I said, I see no difference between Stella's early work and my own.

PS: *I agree, but you make the viewer work harder.*

DS: I didn't think that I was making the viewer do more than the viewer would naturally be doing anyway. I never wanted art to be seen as a puzzle the viewer had to decode. That way simply doesn't have the right feeling for me.

PS: You put more demands on the viewer's attention than early Stella, which people were supposed to experience in a flash.

DS: But I don't think I really did. That was a misleading thing— an assumption similar to calling abstract-expressionist painting "action painting." It's a kind of misnomer that creates a blind spot. I don't think that Stella's work was necessarily any faster than anyone else's. It didn't literally take less time to look at.

PS: Oh, I could argue with you on that. I think there's an immediate impact like colliding with something. It's highly overbearing.

DS: Yes, but that's not the same. You could look at it for a long time. Nothing gets in the way of looking at it for a long time. But none of this is really the point. What I'm talking about is the relative relationship of what kind of attention his work required in its time, and that which mine seems to require now.

PS: I think you get Stella's work fast, then you keep looking at it to find out what's wrong with it and there's nothing wrong with it.

DS: What I see when I look at one of Stella's early paintings is the figure of someone who made the decisions that resulted in something looking like that. Not really looking at the thing so much in the formal sense of, you know, black or red, yellow, orange.

PS: The red, yellow, orange—that's the first split second. Then comes . . .

DS: Looking at his work is the imagining or positing the existence of an individual who made the decisions that led to something looking like that.

49

PS: *"Why would I have done that?"*

DS: Yes. If you were a painter, what would you have had to do in your personality to make a painting that looked like that? That's the most interesting part of the work for me.

PS: *In Stella's case, impressive.*

DS: Very. Of course, the feeling in the work has changed. Instead of thinking about someone making something, you find yourself in recent Stella thinking about someone *causing* something to be made. Which is a different feeling, somewhat like an extravagant monarch who causes eccentric architecture to be built. Of course, the point of this was not to render judgment on Stella or to even discuss his aesthetics, but to make a point about what was the non-difference between so-called formal aesthetics and my thinking about what I wanted to do as an artist.

PS: *Back to the theater. What was the first thing you did in the theater?*

DS: I did not have an apprenticeship. I started at the top (laughter). Peter Gordon and Richard Foreman came to me in 1981. Richard was going to direct a play that Kathy Acker had written. It was Kathy's first play. I think that they asked me to be involved in a very calculated way, because they were interested in my work, but also with a kind of calculatedness that could only occur in the theater, because they thought they might be able to attract some funding by having me design the set, or they might be able to sell part of the set afterward to help finance the production. That's the reality of working in the theater and trying to get things produced. I thought it was very amusing, as we all did. Joseph Papp, I think, had originally intended to produce it but turned it down when he saw the script. And it was subsequently turned down by lots of festivals—by the usual festivals in Europe. But there was a neophyte dramaturge in Amsterdam named Friso Haverkamp, a psychoanalyst who really wanted to be involved in the theater. Friso decided to stake his own money on the first production of *Birth of a Poet*, which is a great rarity in Europe, where the government generally pays for avant-garde art. I think he wanted to have a more dangerous and bohemian life, and I think he thought that Kathy was his ticket. He loved it that everyone else hated the play and was definitely gratified by the fact that this was going to give him more of a chance to fly in the face of Dutch conventionality than anything else he could get his hands on at that moment. I spent a very long time meditating on the script and listening to the score, responding with images that I thought for whatever reason emotionally rhymed. I didn't know anything about what could or could not be done physically. I had no experience in the theater. I had never set foot on a stage. I didn't have any idea what it took to get a piece of scenery from stage left to stage right, or how much money it took to build that piece of scenery. I think that was a very good state of mind to be in for the first production. In other words, I wasn't thinking about it from the inside of the theater. I was thinking about it very much the way I think about paintings, in terms of what it was that I, as a member of the audience, wanted to see when I read the script or heard the score.

PS: *The scale of the '85 production at the Brooklyn Academy of Music was awesome.*

DS: Yes, at this remove I can't believe the number of images we created. I'm sure I will never do anything like it again. The first production in Rotterdam [two years prior to the Brooklyn production] was a sketch by comparison. Even so, it was a very large undertaking for a provincial theater. The play itself was different than what was seen in Brooklyn. It was a little bit shorter. The music was trimmer. Actually, the play as a theatrical experience may have been better in Holland, although decor-wise the Dutch production was a sketch and the Brooklyn production was definitive.

PS: *It bombed in Brooklyn.*

BIRTH OF THE POET, performance, Brooklyn Academy of Music.
Director: Richard Foreman. Libretto: Kathy Acker. Music: Peter Gordon.

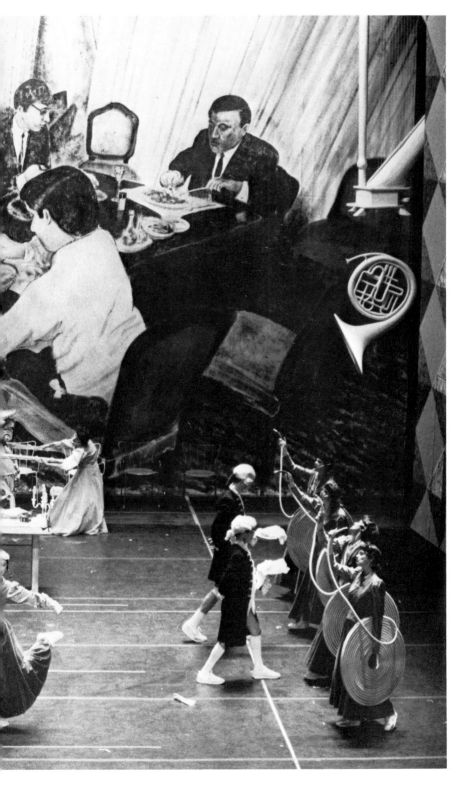

Sets and costumes: David Salle, December 1985.
Photo: Copyright Jean Kallina, 1986.

DS: The play, as a piece of theater, was like watching human suffering. It was too bad; I continue to think the play is quite interesting and I still defend it, although I'm not blind to its flaws.

PS: *So, then between these two productions you started to . . .*

DS: Between the two productions of *Birth of a Poet* I began to occupy stages in my imagination in a way that I hadn't before. I don't know if that's the same thing as taking it seriously or not. But as we've said earlier in this talk, there are certain natural connections between what I had already been doing in painting and what one wanted to see or feel on the stages. For example, in Rotterdam there were certain things, certain moments like the backdrop of Ethel and Robert Scull eating dinner coming down and the actors coming out in their Elizabethan period costumes with garden hoses. The music, a kind of disco approximation of Persian court music, and Richard's beautifully exaggerated silent-movie staging were working all together. Something real was created. Something as palpable as the other art experiences we've been talking about. It was created at that moment and it was something that you could take away with you. That convinced me that this was something to pursue.

PS: *What's the title of the one you're working on currently?*

DS: The Elizabethan Phrasing of the Late Albert Ayler.[4]

PS: *Well, certainly, the one you did,* The Mollino Room, *with Baryshnikov at the Kennedy Center and at Lincoln Center, was wonderful, and I gather a hit with audiences and a washout with critics.*

DS: Well, the American Ballet Theatre audiences were a bit strange, a bit hard to pin down, but, yes, it did seem as though the ballet was successful with the audiences. The ballet press was mixed, at best. The more powerful establishment critics were much more negative than some of the provincial critics and maverick publications. But, on the whole, let's say they were less than appreciative. There were some extremely positive reviews, using words like "thrilling" and "fresh." The point is, those are the kinds of words that weren't used at *The New York Times*, and so people began to form the impression that the piece was a flop because they didn't read about it in the *Times* in that way, in the right way. I'm not sure we really want to go into the whole subject of the nonexistence of critical discourse in America at this moment. I mean, I don't know if you want to broach that depressing subject. I don't know if I'm really up to it.

PS: Well, one of the things people responded badly to was the idea of dancing to Nichols and May.

DS: It's usually a bad idea to have to explain a joke.[5] But the Nichols and May routine was not simply about its ostensible subject—a Jewish boy, a male nurse or whatever people took offense to. It was "about" improvisation, the making of humor—that is, *meaning*—before an audience in an unexpected way. That seemed to us to be quite a beautiful score to dance to, both in terms of rhythm and timbre, and it created a metaphor for creativity. But the *Times* critics and others saw the routine as literal content only, which is how they view all of life, so it was condemned as sexist and even racist. I'm sure that twenty years from now people won't believe this took place.

That kind of pathetic fallacy, exemplified by the *Times*, the *Voice, Art in America, Newsweek*, just about everyone—even Arlene Croce—reads meaning solely from the behavior of the *characters* in a work instead of the whole network of coordinates inside and outside the work that constitutes its meaning. I mean there is just not the perceptual equipment out there to take these things in. That Nichols and May, with their sheer creative brilliance, could have been reduced to a sign for *gender roles* makes me want to laugh and cry. There are actually many amusing stories connected with the press reception to *Mollino Room*. For example, Misha's costume had a painted rendering of Brancusi's *The Sleeping*

Muse on his shirt. It was a very poignant image that worked with the solitude and strength of his role. Anna Kisselgoff went on record in the *Times* by referring to the design as a smirking fish! Not only did the ballet world not know or care who Carlo Mollino was,[6] they couldn't recognize Brancusi.

PS: Let's talk about critics.

DS: It seems as though one could divide critics up into two groups: those who have an idea about how art comes to have meaning, and stemming from that idea, a set of aesthetic principles by which to evaluate the relative success or failure of something, whether it's a painting or a ballet; and those who write consumer-guide-type journalism. And I must say as an aside that my involvement with things on stages, and more specifically with the Armitage Ballet, has given me a new access to ire that had been more or less becalmed in regards to my painting work—my life as a painter in the past few years—as my own appetite for the adversarial position vis-à-vis my own work in the world diminished. But being involved with the ballet company has given me anew feelings of confusion and frustration with criticism in our time. Anyway, about there being in my mind two types of critics, there are the critics who try to establish a relationship with a *work,* and then there are the *complaining* critics. The journalistic critics in general, or I should say the *complaining* critics, reduce everything to a sign, and then complain bitterly because everything has been reduced to a sign. This is the essential antagonism between artists and critics, really. I don't see how it can ever go away when the critics have one eye on the audience. That is their authoritarianism disguised as populism. They too want to be loved. I believe that we as artists are *not* reducing things to signs; we are making things which have very specific appearances and which can have complex and sometimes fragile meanings. The complaining critics want to level everything out with ideology, or sarcasm, or social snobbery, or lousy writing, or whatever, while decrying the leveled-out, nonidiosyncratic culture they have helped shape. Artists want to cast wider nets *and* be more specific simultaneously. The complaining critics hold on to an image of themselves as cultural myth-debunkers, when of course that position itself is largely mythic unless we talk about specific people in specific epochs like Mark Twain. These people are just helping to sell newspapers by creating the false impression of intimacy, only in this case with culture. Another weird point of confusion among some of the complaining critics is that they want to be postmodernists and leftists simultaneously, when a real post-modernist sensibility would obviate or eclipse that stupid watchdog attitude toward art and its economics. And beyond that, there's an idea among these journalistic critics that they seem to feel their job is to warn people away from things that they might not understand instead of helping people to understand those things. There are numerous exceptions to this critique of criticism: the people who have managed through hard work and good spirit to break through this terrible enclosure of meaninglessness that criticism is in—and the mean-spiritedness of criticism toward the works of art that it criticizes. But while we're talking about the negative side, I would say that the type of writing which most inflames my antag-onism and sense of outrage, particularly when it's directed at Kar-ole's work, contains this feeling, this idea that the audience is like the wolf boy of Aveyron. The audience is like their wolf boy; it doesn't have access to a language of its own and as a result it doesn't have access to feeling. I would say this attitude is epito-mized by the dance criticism in *The New York Times*, where one always finds a tone of pseudodeduction, as if to say that one's eyes and ears are not already connected to one's mind. As if all one can do is to assume this phony detachment out of which one can make "deductions" based on so-called empirical observation, which of course is ludicrous because the critics are heavily biased. One last thing along this line. I don't understand why it is that people charged with discussing works of art in the public eye, the critics of our great newspapers, have chosen to take a tone which is so defensively baffled by things that are serious and have a high level of ambition, of serious aesthetic ambition. The kinds of contem-porary works that are held before the public as having meaning and levels of correspondence with life are the works that are the most metonymical, to go back to the earlier problem of late modernism: that is to say, the works that are merely stand-ins or the works which have on them, as it were, names for experience in life rather than things which create experience in life or allow for the creation of experience in life. Why our critics have opted for the unreal over the real is itself, I'm sure, symptomatic of something much larger. Actually, what irritates one the most is their utter predictability.

PS: Well, the critics have a problem knowing who they write for. There is a fragmentation between the inner circle of the audience for artists, defined by artists and collectors, say, and the next line of reception. Do you find the perceptions in Europe any more acute?

DS: Perhaps more acute but no less wrongheaded, because they have also posited a certain set of ideas about the audience which I think are offensive, especially in the ballet world. Ideas about what's "avant-garde" or "unconventional"—that kind of nonsense. They are not even very observant, and, as said earlier, the writing gives a tone of almost scientific data-gathering-like detachment from which deductions are made, while their ability to actually visually discriminate between thing A and thing B is very dim. All these dim little Descartes! Decrying fashion while following it helplessly because they have *no context*, only a fragmented history and a provincial sense of causality. This is of course why they are so condescending to the audience, because they have no context for anything themselves and can't believe that anyone else might be able to form one.

PS: There has been tremendous resistance to your work in Europe. How do you explain that?

DS: Maybe they just don't like the way it looks. There is in Europe always a feeling of the problem of art being not aesthetic but political; that is to say, the problems of criticism in Europe—and also of art—are related to knowing what something is supposed to stand for as opposed to sensing what it actually is. Certainly in Europe one senses—and I don't know whether this is good or bad —a much stronger residue of the modernist desire for utopian revolution. This is particularly true in dance, but it's also true in painting. What is interesting is that the work which has been most easily assimilated into the European intellectual treadmill is conceptual art, which, even though it has a utopian residue, is actually the most elitist and hyperformalist art to have been made, in my opinion.

PS: *Well, it's the kind of art that calls for and enforces the activity of the socialist institutions of the culture. There is also a powerful strain of anticommercialism in Europe.*

DS: Well, of course there is some horror in Europe at the idea of working for a living to begin with; it is social anathema to them. And, in my opinion, this idea is a complete sham. It's an example of the general avoidance of the reality of living, which is that people work, work for money. You know, the irony is that the people who have this objection to art are invariably leftist-type people who should more than others be involved in the reality of the economics of working. They all still get money from home.

PS: *How do you cope with this, with all the negative response to your work?*

DS: Oh, it goes from amusement to rage to indifference, back and forth. Karole and I discuss this all the time because, as a performer, she's more directly affected by it and sometimes discouraged by it. If you have to make your work literally in front of the public, and you have these very intransigent and arbitrary kinds of responses in the public press, I think it's much harder on you. I think it's also disorienting when you have the communicativeness of your work verified before your eyes by your audience—and then you

BLUE PAPER, 1986. Acrylic, oil/canvas; 108″ × 174″ (3).
Collection of Beaubourg Museum, Paris. Photo: Zindman/Fremont.

have the same work dealt with as something incomprehensible in the next day's paper. The discrepancy is disconcerting. As far as dance is concerned, we can generally assume that whatever appears in the press will be the exact opposite of our experience of something. That's how great the discrepancy is. I don't really have to contend with that; in addition to having hostile remarks made about my work, which comes with the territory, I've been blessed with the serious interest and attention of a number of people who write about art extremely well. There is some shared context. I've only been talking about a certain segment—there are many others; some are wonderful. The point I've been trying to make in discussing this is really not to complain about the treatment that either I or Karole has suffered at the hands of the critics. The point I was trying to make is that the people who write for the media, because they *are* the media, those who get paid to deliver, dead or alive, the new art to a vaguely curious audience, are just playing out the latest manifestation of the residual antagonism between avant-garde art and the wider culture, only kind of inside out. You know, at a certain point, one simply has to ignore it.

I V

K E E P I N G   G O I N G

PS: We started out talking about your coming to New York, when the only question that seemed entertainable was how to be an artist at all. Ten years later, is that question settled for you?

DS: I have to answer in a roundabout way—to try to describe a little bit a peculiar chain of events. Contrary to stories about early success, I feel like I'm just now beginning to do my work. It was a very long time coming—the necessary levels of integration to make it work were hard for me to achieve and I feel like I'm still very much trying to achieve them. In one way, I "did my work" a long time ago, while I was still in school, really. I intuitively arrived at many of the things my work would be about and which, apparently, continue to interest the next generation, albeit in a drier way: the thinking about doubles, the model, presentation, the a-priori-ness of things, the obligatory, uses of style—all of that I embarked on in a primitive way while in school. And I felt for years, as my work sort of went nowhere, very deeply about a kind of loss—a misspent kind of time. I had the feeling of knowing I had seen "it"—glimpsed it but hadn't objectified it in a successful way. Then I thought it was more or less over—you know, like I had been there, I had seen the work but hadn't made it—and there is no worse feeling in life than knowing you didn't do what you could have done. I felt the moment had passed. I had done my work to a certain level, a kind of basic research level, and no one was interested; it was too marginal, and I didn't have the energy, partly because the ideas themselves can be enervating, to work with to find a greater, more realized form. This was going on over a period of years and I had, in effect, practically lost interest in "it." I just felt that I probably wouldn't have a career as an artist. I had said what I had to say, but in a very small voice. In fact, I just simply wasn't working very hard, wasn't confronting the visual fact of my work. It is ironical, because in one sense I preceded my own generation in terms of outlining the material, but in another more real sense I was on the sidelines, not even very attentive, when my generation of artists got under steam. It's funny, isn't it; I suppose I had been more adversely affected by isolation and cynicism than I realized. And again, it's almost like the late seventies for me—I can *see* something big in the middle distance, but I don't have in my being the necessary levels of integration to really visualize and externalize it. I feel like I have so much work yet to be done and now I don't know if I have the stamina I had ten years ago.

PS: *Well, nothing stays the same, and if you're not growing, you're declining.*

DS: You have to be very alert to that and to the American notion of publicity and celebrity, the decline of intellectual life in America, the absence of criticism—and of course human nature, fatigue, laziness, having said what you wanted to say, all the forces that can join to make that the thing that happens. One thing I should add is that I think that decline is actually more prevalent in Europe than in America. I don't think in America you'd find the situation of a Daniel Buren who twenty years later can still make headlines with vertical stripes of a certain width. What we're talking about is invention—seeing how far your invention will take you aesthetically, how big a theme it can encompass—and contrary to postmodern theory I very much believe in invention as a large part of the challenge. Of course, in my generation invention didn't mean a single signature style, and as a result what's "invented" is sometimes hard to pin down. The large answer to your question about keeping going has to do with that: can you invent something, some way of speaking in the pictures, more than once? I certainly hope I can. As I said, I feel it coming.

PS: *Maybe this raises the question of whether the artist creates the age or the age creates the artist. In many different ways an artist becomes the tool of the moment, and a tool is dropped when the job is done.*

DS: There are different kinds of artists. There are artists who work in a kind of pure gift way; I think of Rauschenberg in that sense. From '55 to '65, let's say, just pure gift. Pure inspiration, and after that it's just kind of something else. Whereas with artists like Jasper Johns, it's much slower, a much more gradual kind of incremental mastering this and then mastering that and then putting the two together and mastering the third thing, very slow, very gradual, very incremental and deliberate.

PS: *One of my favorite quotes about art is almost too bland to quote, but it keeps resonating for me. Morandi said about Chardin that he painted a world that interested him personally. As opposed to somebody like Rauschenberg who just gives and—*

DS: He gives and he also wants to be loved on a public level; that's his artistic makeup. I think that wanting public love is very problematic, and of course part of being an artist. But I don't think that painting something that interests one deeply guarantees anything. I can think of artists who are totally absorbed in what interests them personally who make art that's not very interesting. Anyway, why would we necessarily be interested in what interests them personally?

PS: *It's a better bet for longevity.*

DS: I'm more interested in an artist like de Chirico, who's sort of beyond all that on the one hand and more engaged on the other. You know, his work is problematic. Morandi had no faults, and his record is clean and the pictures are beautiful and I've always liked them, but I never think about them. With de Chirico, obviously what he did interested him personally, but it was also tied up with all kinds of crazy ideas about the world and thinking

65

and the public and whether he was loved or wasn't loved and full of hatreds for the world and settling of scores. It gives his work a lot of character.

PS: So he keeps alive a lot of questions about how and why to be an artist, but that doesn't make all the paintings good.

DS: Good art over the long haul is more difficult than good art made once. You don't have the same relationship to your life that you did when you started.

DUAL ASPECT PICTURE, 1986.
Acrylic, oil/canvas; 156″ × 117″ (2).
Collection of Ludwig Museum, Cologne.
Photo: Zindman/Fremont.

V

PAINTING'S BODY

PS: *I want to talk about responses to your work. There have been so many that I think one is pretty much obliged to stick with one's own. I know when I first saw your work it was very disturbing to me. As with all things that are new, it probably had to do with reacting to what wasn't there, and it took me awhile to get around to what was. But I've noticed, looking at your work attentively for six years or so, a repeating phenomenon, that of going away from seeing your things extremely stimulated and with vivid memories, and thought processes that seem to continue on their own, but eventually they get attenuated and fall apart, leaving a rather sour residue. If I haven't seen something by you for a while, I can start to think that I'm overliking it, and no matter how many times this happens, it always happens the same way. Then, when I see something new, something good by you, there is an immediate freshening, an immediate dropping away of that mood of depression.*

DS: Generally I think it's good for art to feel overrated when you're not looking at it. That's partly a result of the specificity that we were talking about earlier. It's good to be reminded of it: the part that memory plays in art is very interesting and strange. There is a curious psychological process of rejecting in the memory something that was strong experientially. There is work with the opposite feeling—thinking it's great, and then seeing it and not liking it. But I'm curious about what your sour feeling is, what that's constituted of. I sometimes reject my entire enterprise as having been the wrong one. I feel that my work might have got stuck in a minor key. I don't know what the right one would have been; I feel like this simply was the wrong thing to have done. I'm not sure that it's different from what artists in general feel periodically, and I don't know if it's related to what you feel.

PS: *Well, maybe in my case it's a rejuvenation of my faith in art, my belief in art's ability to make a difference, which then, under the bombardment of life as it is, comes to seem wrong.*

DS: Oh, you think that's how it goes? As if life as it is overtakes the work, renders the work kind of wrongheaded, or—

PS: *Well, a disappointment, a sense of possibilities which time reveals to be dubious.*

DS: What happens with other people's work when you haven't seen it for a while and you think about it in your mind's eye?

PS: *Well, many artists supply a very reliable kind of pleasure, that is always there, but I feel something similar with other artists who mean a great deal to me. Like Jasper Johns, or Bruce Nauman, and Anselm Kiefer.*

DS: With some of those artists I also feel there's something that I'd like to be finished with, a feeling of wanting to be finished with it, and then you realize that you're not finished with it yet, and it's frustrating.

PS: *Or it's not finished with you. I think you're also the kind of artist who tends to take over, almost to replace the subjectivity of anyone who gives the work complete attention. And in a certain way it's exciting to be relieved of one's own familiar, boring subjectivity, but in another way it's a kind of violation. In the past you've said things about the paintings looking at the viewer, and that's a very ambivalent relationship. Also there's a calculated or at least conscious outrage in your imagery, and in your way of presenting it, that seems to demand a response which your work simultaneously makes very difficult. I mean, the excitement and the frustration are simultaneous. You know what I'm talking about?*

DS: I don't know if I do or not.

PS: *I think your work has been important in my life because the whole issue of the importance of art is central to my life, and you make it possible to experience the problems. There's an edge where everything's at issue.*

DS: I wonder what it would be like if I made pictures with images that were very neutral. I'm not certain that's ever really the case. Like flags and targets—it's a myth that they're neutral.

PS: No, targets are very powerful devices and you don't get much more powerful in terms of devices than the flag.

DS: But for so long there was this art-myth that they were neutral. I've often thought it would be interesting if people could look at my images as neutral as well, instead of assuming that they're charged. I do believe that there will come a time in which this so-called disturbing interest in my work will be seen as a condition of the work, much as the stripes in Stella's early work, for which he was attacked, are now seen as a *condition* of the work, how the work looks, not the thing which determines its quality. But the point is to look at the whole painting, whatever kind of painting it is, and not look at one thing in the painting and describe the painting's value in terms of that one thing. It's like not having learned anything about the relationship between form and content. As in all classical painting, this is not the problem, not the issue. The other thing to mention is that there are things in my paintings and there are things in the world and the two things are not the same—even though one might look like the other. Nudes in paintings are not the same as nudes in the world. It's their relationship that's interesting. The other thing to say is that the specificity of the poses in my paintings is much different really than that of the poses one sees in pornography. The poses of women in my paintings are actually more about sympathetic identification. Some people, of course, may never believe that.

PS: It becomes interesting, then, to gauge the difference of an inch in leg openings. One of the things throughout your work is that the erotic becomes graded very precisely.

71

DS: It is germane to everything we were talking about; the elements in painting—whether my paintings or someone else's paintings—are always *very specific*. When people look at my pictures and try to describe them, they tend to generalize and make a list of more or less general attributes. It's the lack of acceptance of certain terms, certain conditions, in new art that makes its relationship with its audience seem confrontational in the short run. It's as if they got their idea of what the painting is over the telephone. One of the things that makes art worth looking at is its absolute specificity, its insistence that even if it kind of looks like pinstripes or pornography or comics, it's *not* that exactly. Those generalized terms are just its *conditions.* Those conditions can seem confrontational in the short run, but they will eventually fall away (as shocking) and be seen for what they are—something which established a field of meaning for a work in a particular way but which is not simply a stand-in for something else it may resemble. *Because they're arrived at in a completely different way.* What people don't see is that for art to be any good, it must have this attitude of surety or of everything already being accepted. That in no way means the work is passive, or is simple, mirroring the culture, which is an astonishingly frequent category mistake one sees in the press.

There has been painting for hundreds of years that wanted to see the interior workings of human beings, in a physical sense. And there has been painting that wanted to examine the exterior mannerisms of human society. Both kinds of paintings have existed side by side for hundreds of years, and I think my paintings have something of both.

PS: *Who would you say is an example of the first kind?*

DS: I would say one of the great painters of the obligatory such as we were talking about earlier and who doesn't shrink from any physical or moral realities is Breughel. I think that there is an idea about the body being the location of human inquiry that one finds in my work, that makes it somehow resonant with much earlier kinds of paintings. I'm not comparing my work to allegorical painting, but you do what you have to do. You don't shrink from it, whether it is reductivist or scatological. And then a bit more recently we have Nauman. The other, the social kind of painting, is exemplified by Watteau, who for me is a divinity.

PS: *The body starts being less interesting with the onset of modernity and the switch to the outside and what's happening. I mean the body becomes markedly less interesting than a locomotive. There is a sense developed by Brice Marden in the late sixties of identity between the skin of the painting and a body. You have a vulnerable surface which is like flesh.*

DS: The contemporary consciousness holds that "I own my body," and my painting's interest in "body" goes against this liberal hubris. It's a little bit like the physical curiosity engendered by war movies. Also, in painting there is the play on the tension of wanting to enter the pictorial space, penetrate the space. Johns has given us an unsurpassable example of the painting as body analogy in *The Dutch Wives.*

PS: *What is a Dutch wife?*

DS: It's a piece of wood with a hole in it used by sailors at sea as a surrogate for women. Hence those little drips on the painting, right below the circles. You could think of it as having set a coffee cup down on the surface of the painting, but you can also think of it another way.

PS: *I think part of the rejuvenation of painting in recent times has been the discovery that it is perhaps the last medium that can be really shocking. There is something about the physicality of it, I guess.*

DS: I think that you have first of all the idea that someone painted it, someone did it.

PS: *Somebody did it alone and in private. And it's unique, like a body.*

DS: The point about the poses in my work is that they are the body in extremes—often seen from strange points of view and spatial orientation. It has more to do with the abstract choreography and angles of vision than with pornographic narrative. They are not voyeuristic in the sense that Eric's depictions of intimate family scenes are voyeuristic, because they're not candid—i.e., they're specifically posed in order to be seen that way.

PS: I think in general people choose not to look at paintings for the very reasons we're giving. And the technology is still utterly primitive. The existence of paintings as unique handmade objects flies in the face of the twentieth century.

DS: I don't really think about that very much. I mean, in a sense, the twentieth century flies in the face of the twentieth century. In a way it's not unlike performance, because although always present, it's the result of some physical effort that's gone. I don't really like to think about what the viewers think. But I have an idea that it takes a great deal of looking at painting to feel palpably that thing you were just talking about. That feeling that you'll never see anything else in your life exactly like that. It's an idea for me which has always been one of the most poignant. . . .

N O T E S

1. By 1982, Fischl, Immendorff and Salle were all affiliated with the same galleries in New York and Cologne, Mary Boone and Michael Werner.

2. By 1980, the Sonnabend Gallery was representing A. R. Penck in America.

3. po-mo: slang for postmodern.

4. The full-length ballet *The Elizabethan Phrasing of the Late Albert Ayler*, choreography by Karole Armitage with sets and costumes by David Salle, received its world premiere at the Statsshoulberg Theatre in Eindhoven, the Netherlands, in September 1986 and subsequently toured Europe, the U.S. and Canada, opening at the Brooklyn Academy of Music in November 1987.

5. *The Mollino Room* (1986), Kennedy Center, Washington, D.C., and the Metropolitan Opera House, New York. Choreography by Karole Armitage, featuring Mikhail Baryshnikov. The score for the thirty-minute ballet consisted of two different Hindemith compositions sandwiched around a 1960 recording of Mike Nichols and Elaine May improvising a routine called "My Son the Nurse."

6. Carlo Mollino (1905–1975), Italian architect, designer of buildings, interiors, furniture, cars, airplanes. Seminal figure in the evolution of postwar European modern style. Often noted for evocative juxtapositions of period styles (materials, patterns, shapes) with highly original formal and structural inventions.

APPENDIX

SOLO EXHIBITIONS

1976   Artists Space, New York, New York.

1977   Foundation de Appel, Amsterdam, Netherlands.
       The Kitchen, New York, New York.

1978   Foundation Corps de Garde, Groningen, Netherlands.

1979   Gagosian/Nosei-Weber Gallery, New York, New York.
       The Kitchen, New York, New York.

1980   Foundation de Appel, Amsterdam, Netherlands.
       Anina Nosei Gallery, New York, New York.
       Galerie Bischofberger, Zürich, Switzerland.

1981   Mary Boone Gallery, New York, New York.
       Larry Gagosian Gallery, Los Angeles, California.
       Lucio Amelio Gallery, Naples, Italy.

1982   Mario Diacono Gallery, Rome, Italy.
       Mary Boone Gallery and Leo Castelli Gallery,
           New York, New York.
       Galerie Bischofberger, Zürich, Switzerland.
       Anthony D'Offay Gallery, London, England.

1983   Akira Ikeda Gallery, Tokyo, Japan.
       Ronald Greenberg Gallery, St. Louis, Missouri.
       Museum Boymans-van Beuningen, Rotterdam,
           Netherlands.

Mary Boone Gallery, New York, New York.
Castelli Graphics, New York, New York.
Galerie Ascan Crone, Hamburg, West Germany.
Galerie Schellman and Kluser, Munich, West Germany.
Addison Gallery of American Art, Andover,
 Massachusetts.

1984　Leo Castelli Gallery, New York, New York.
Mario Diacono Gallery, Rome, Italy.
Galerie Bischofberger, Zürich, Switzerland.

1985　Texas Gallery, Houston, Texas.
Galerie Daniel Templon, Paris, France.
Mary Boone Gallery, New York, New York.
Galerie Michael Werner, Cologne, West Germany.
Donald Young Gallery, Chicago, Illinois.

1986　Leo Castelli Gallery, New York, New York.
Mario Diacono Gallery, Boston, Massachusetts.
Castelli Graphics, New York, New York.
Museum am Ostwall, Dortmund, West Germany.
Institute of Contemporary Art, Philadelphia,
 Pennsylvania.
Institute of Contemporary Art, Boston,
 Massachusetts.

1987　The Whitney Museum of American Art, New York, New
 York.
Museum of Contemporary Art, Los Angeles,
 California.
Art Gallery of Ontario, Toronto, Canada.
Contemporary Art Museum, Chicago, Illinois.
Mary Boone Gallery, New York, New York.
Fruitmarket Gallery, Edinburgh, Scotland.
Spiral/Wacoal Art Center, Tokyo, Japan.

GROUP EXHIBITIONS

1979   "Masters of Love," 80 Langton Street,
         San Francisco, California.
       "Imitation of Life," Joseloff Gallery, Hartford
         Art School, Hartford, Connecticut.

1980   "Après le Classicisme," Musée d'Art et Industrie
         et Maison de la Culture, St.-Etienne, France.
       "Horror Pleni: Give me time to look, Pictures
         in New York Today," Padiglione d'Art
         Contemporanea, Milan, Italy.
       "Illustration and Allegory," Brooke Alexander
         Gallery, New York, New York.

1981   "Young Americans," Allen Memorial Art Museum,
         Oberlin, Ohio.
       "Westkunst: Heute," Museum der Stadt Köln, Cologne,
         West Germany.
       "Figures, Forms, and Expressions," Albright-Knox
         Museum, Buffalo, New York.
       "Body Language," Hayden Gallery, MIT, Cambridge,
         Massachusetts.
       "Aspects of Post Modernism," Squibb Gallery,
         Princeton, New Jersey.
       "U.S. Art Now," Göteborgs Konstmoseum, Göteborg,
         Sweden; Bard College, Annandale, New York.

1982   "Focus on the Figure: Twenty Years," The Whitney
         Museum of American Art, New York, New York.

"The Anxious Edge," Walker Art Center, Minneapolis, Minnesota.

"Castelli and His Artists," Museum of Contemporary Art, La Jolla, California.

"Art and the Media," Renaissance Society, Chicago, Illinois.

"Avanguardia Transavanguardia," Mura Aureliane, Rome, Italy.

"74th American Exhibition," The Chicago Art Institute, Chicago, Illinois.

"Dokumenta 7," Kassel, West Germany.

"La Biennale di Venezia," Venice, Italy.

"The Pressure to Paint," Marlborough Gallery, New York, New York.

"Avanguardia Transavanguardia," Gallery Civica, Modena, Italy.

"Body Language," The Fort Worth Art Museum, Fort Worth, Texas.

"Zeitgeist," Berlin, West Germany.

"The Expressionist Image: American Art from Pollock to Today," Sidney Janis Gallery, New York, New York.

"New York Now," Kestner-Gesellschaft, Hannover, West Germany.

"New Figuration in America," Milwaukee Art Museum, Milwaukee, Wisconsin.

1983   "En International Samling," Stiftelsen Karlsvik 10, Stockholm, Sweden.

"The Whitney Biennial," The Whitney Museum of American Art, New York, New York.

"Directions 1983," The Hirshhorn Museum, Washington, D.C.

"From Minimalism to Expressionism," The Whitney Museum of American Art, New York, New York.

"Tendencias en Nueva York," Crystal Palace, Madrid, Spain.

"São Paulo Bienalle," São Paulo, Brazil.
"New Art," The Tate Gallery, London, England.
"Back to the USA," Kunstmuseum Luzern, Lucerne,
    Switzerland.

1984 "New Painting," Krannert Art Museum, Champaign,
        Illinois.
     "New Art," Musée d'Art Contemporain, Montréal,
        Canada.
     "An International Survey of Contemporary Painting
        and Sculpture," Museum of Modern Art, New York,
        New York.
     "The Human Condition": SFMAA Biennial III," San
        Francisco Museum of Modern Art, San Francisco,
        California.
     "Kapelle am Wegesrand," La Paloma, Hamburg, West
        Germany.
     "Aspekte Amerikanischer Kunst der Gegenwart," Neue
        Galerie Sammlung Ludwig, Aachen, West Germany.
     "The Restoration of Painterly Figuration: Painting
        Now," Kitakyushu Municipal Museum of Art,
        Kitakyushu, Japan.
     "Polke, Salle, Clemente," Contemporary Art Gallery,
        Seibu Department Store, Tokyo, Japan.
     "Content," The Hirshhorn Museum, Washington, D.C.
     "Ouverture," Castello di Rivoli, Torino, Italy.

1985 "The Whitney Biennial," The Whitney Museum of
        American Art, New York, New York.
     "XIIIᵉ Biennale de Paris," Grande Halle du Parc
        de la Villette, Paris, France.
     "New York '85," ARCAA, Marseilles, France.
     "Carnegie International," Museum of Art, Carnegie
        Institute, Pittsburgh, Pennsylvania.

1986 "An American Renaissance, Painting and Sculpture
        Since 1940," Museum of Art, Fort Lauderdale, Florida.

"Biennale of Sydney," Sydney, Australia.
"Ooghoogte, 50 jaar later," Stedelijk Van Abbemuseum, Eindhoven, Netherlands.
"Europe/America," Ludwig Museum, Cologne, West Germany.
"Avant-Garde in the Eighties," Los Angeles County Museum, Los Angeles, California.
"Prospect 86," Frankfurter Kunstverein, Frankfurt, West Germany.

1987   "L'Époque, La Mode, La Morale, La Passion," Centre Georges Pompidou, Paris, France.

BIBLIOGRAPHY

Burgin, Richard. "The Impact of Conceptual Art at Project Inc." *The Boston Globe*, September 17, 1974.

Baker, Kenneth. "It's the Thought That Counts." *The Boston Phoenix*, September 24, 1974.

Askey, Ruth. "On Video: Banality, Sex, Cooking." *Artweek*, August 8, 1975.

Robbe, Lon de Vries. "David Salle." *Museums Journal*, September 1976.

Patton, Phil. "Other Voices, Other Rooms: The Rise of the Alternative Space." *Art in America*, Summer 1977.

Bleckner, Ross. "Transcendent Anti-fetishism." *Artforum*, March 1979.

Lawson, Thomas. "On Pictures, A Manifesto." *Flash Art*, April 1979.

Robinson, Walter. "Art Strategies for the '80s: A Guide to What's Hot." *Adix*, October 1979.

Zimmer, William. "Who Puts Women on a Pedestal?" *Soho Weekly News*, November 15, 1979.

Rickey, Carrie. "Voice Choices: David Salle." *The Village Voice*, November 21, 1979.

Tatransky, Valentin. "Intelligence and the Desire to Draw: On David Salle." *Real Life*, November 1979.

Lawson, Thomas. "David Salle." *Flash Art*, January/February 1980, p. 37.

Tatransky, Valentin. "David Salle." *Arts Magazine*, February 1980, p. 37.

Robinson, Walter. "David Salle at Gagosian/Nosei-Weber." *Art in America*, March 1980, p. 117.

Oliva, Achille Bonito. "The Bewildered Image." *Flash Art*, March/April 1980. (Illus.: *Untitled*, b&w.)

Pincus-Witten, Robert. "Entries: Big History: Little History." *Arts Magazine*, April 1980, p. 183.

———. "Entries: Palimpsest and Pentimenti." *Arts Magazine*, June 1980, pp. 128–131.

Salle, David. "Images That Understand Us." *Journal*, June/July 1980, pp. 41–44.

Rickey, Carrie. "Advance to Rear Guard." *The Village Voice*, August 27, 1980, p. 66.

———. "Naïve Nouveau and Its Malcontents." *Flash Art*, Summer 1980, pp. 36–39.

Tatransky, Valentin. "Illustration and Allegory." *Arts Magazine,* September 1980, p. 4.

Phillips, Deborah. "Illustration and Allegory." *Arts Magazine,* September 1980, p. 25.

Yoskowitz, Robert. "Group Show." *Arts Magazine,* September 1980, p. 30.

Pincus-Witten, Robert. "Entries: If Even in Fractions." *Arts Magazine,* September 1980, p. 119.

Wohlfert, Lee. "Young Artists New Yorkers Are Talking About." *Town and Country,* September 1980, pp. 199–207. (Illus.: *Always Render Explicit,* b&w.)

Simon, Joan. "Double Takes." *Art in America,* October 1980, pp. 113–117.

Hess, Elizabeth. "Barefoot Girls with Cheek Glass." *The Village Voice,* November 19–25, 1980, p. 93.

Isaacs, Florence. "New Artists for the '80's." *Prime Time,* November 1980.

Tomkins, Calvin. "The Art World." *The New Yorker,* December 22, 1980, pp. 78–80.

Salle, David. *Cover Magazine,* Winter 1980/1981, pp. 52–53.

Smith, Roberta. "Separation Anxieties." *The Village Voice,* March 18, 1981, p. 78.

Olander, William. "Young Americans." *Dialogue,* March/April 1981, pp. 42–44. (Illus.: *Rainy Night in Rubber City,* b&w.)

Lawson, Thomas. "Switching Channels." *Flash Art,* March/April 1981, pp. 20–22.

Zanetti, Paolo Serra. "New York—New Work." *Meta,* March/April 1981.

Knox, Marion. "Letter from New York." *Transatlantic,* April 4, 1981, pp. 70–73.

Christy, George. "The Great Life." *The Hollywood Reporter,* April 24, 1981.

Wilson, William. "David Salle." *Los Angeles Times,* April 24, 1981, part VI, p. 9.

Drohojowska, Hunter. "Pick of the Week." *Los Angeles Weekly,* April 24–30, 1981.

Siegel, Jeanne. "David Salle: Interpretation of Image." *Arts Magazine,* April 1981, pp. 94–95.

Smith, Roberta. "Biennial Blues." *Art in America,* April 1981, pp. 92–101.

Knight, Christopher. "The Medium Cool Art of David Salle." *Los Angeles Herald Examiner,* May 3, 1981, p. E6. (Illus.: *Savagery and Misrepresentation,* b&w.)

Collins, Dan, and Hicks, Emily. "Meaning Through Disparity." *Artweek,* May 9, 1981, p. 3. (Illus.: *Savagery and Misrepresentation,* b&w.)

Pincus-Witten, Robert. "Entries: Sheer Grunge." *Arts Magazine,* May 1981, pp. 93–97. (Illus.: *Archer's House,* b&w.)

Lawson, Thomas. "David Salle at Mary Boone." *Artforum,* May 1981, pp. 71–72. (Illus.: *Long Intervals of Time and Years,* b&w.)

Kiefer, Geraldine Wojino. "This Is Where I Live." *Northern Ohio Live*, May 1981, pp. 8–9.

Meyer, Ruth K. "Young Americans: Wish Fulfillment." *Dialogue*, May/June 1981, pp. 6–9.

Marzorati, Gerald. "Art Picks: Salle/Schnabel." *The Soho News*, June 24, 1981, p. 36.

McClelland, Elizabeth. "Rhetoric Beefs Up 'Young Americans.' " *New Art Examiner*, June 1981, p. 5.

Ricard, Rene. "Not About Julian Schnabel." *Artforum*, Summer 1981, pp. 74–80.

Staff. *Museums Journal*, No. 3, 1981. (Illus.: *We'll Shake the Bag*, cover, c.)

Ratcliff, Carter. "Westkunst: David Salle." *Flash Art*, Summer 1981, pp. 33–34.

Levine, Sherrie. "David Salle." *Flash Art*, Summer 1981, p. 34.

Salle, David. "Post-Modernism." *Real Life*, Summer 1981, pp. 4–10.

Zimmer, William. "Art Picks: Andy Warhol." *The Soho News*, September 30, 1981, p. 28.

Marzorati, Gerald. "Art Picks." *The Soho News*, September 30, 1981, p. 30.

Zimmer, William. "Dark Continents." *The Soho News*, September 30, 1981, p. 78.

Yoskowitz, Robert. "David Salle." *Arts Magazine*, September 1981, p. 31.

Armstrong, Richard. "Cologne: Heute." *Artforum*, September 1981, pp. 83–86.

Trucco, Terry. "Sensations of the Year." *Portfolio*, September/October 1981, pp. 42–47.

Anderson, Alexandra. "Schnabel's Sally." *Portfolio*, September/October 1981, p. 6.

Schjeldahl, Peter. "David Salle Interview." *Journal*, September/October 1981, pp. 15–21.

Lawson, Thomas. "Last Exit: Painting." *Artforum*, October 30, 1981, pp. 40–47.

Hammond, Pamela. "David Salle at Larry Gagosian." *Images and Issues*, Fall 1981, pp. 60–61.

Lawson, Thomas. "Too Good to Be True." *Real Life*, Autumn 1981, pp. 3–7.

Salle, David. "David Salle." *File Magazine*, Vol. 5, No. 2.

Frueh, Joanna. "Young Americans at the Allen Memorial Art Museum." *Art in America*, October 1981, p. 151.

Oliva, Achille Bonito. "The International Trans-Avantgarde." *Flash Art*, October/November 1981, pp. 36–43.

Deitch, Jeffrey. "Who Has the Power?" *Flash Art*, October/November 1981, pp. 46–47.

Howell, George. "Artists Take Up the Human Form." *Buffalo Evening News*, November 15, 1981.

Bannon, Anthony. " 'Figures' Is Bold and Bright." *Buffalo Evening News,*
November 25, 1981, p. B8.

Marmer, Nancy. "Isms on the Rhine." *Art in America,* November 1981,
pp. 112–113.

Plagens, Peter. "The Academy of the Bad." *Art in America,* November 1981,
pp. 11–17. (Illus.: *Bold New Thesis,* p.11, b&w.)

Ratcliff, Carter. "European Imports." *Ambassador,* November 1981, pp. 53–54.

Anderson, Ali. "Around the Block: Avarice and Arrivistes in Soho." *Art and
Auction,* November 1981, pp. 12–14.

Tomkins, Calvin. "The Art World: An End to Chauvinism." *The New Yorker,*
December 7, 1981, pp. 146–154.

Levin, Kim. "Rhine Wine." *The Village Voice,* December 16–22, 1981, p. 126.

Perrault, John. "Time Running Out for Spaces." *Soho News,* December 22,
1981, p. 60.

Diacono, Mario. "Man with a Camera." Self-published, December 1981.

Schjeldahl, Peter. "Absent-minded Female Nude on Bed (For David Salle)."
Artforum, December 1981, p. 49.

Gintz, Claude. "Une Saison à New York." *Artistes,* Winter 1981, pp. 27–35.
(Illus.: *Calling Rather Than a Career,* b&w.)

Brooks, Rosetta. "The Art Machine: Editorial." *ZG Magazine,* No. 3, pp. 1–2.

Caroli, Flavio. "Magico Primario." *Gruppo Editorial Fabbri,* 1982.

Oliva, Achille Bonito. "Avanguardia Transavanguardia." *Electa,* Milan, 1982.

Owens, Craig. "Back to the Studio." *Art in America,* January 1982,
pp. 99–107.

Haime, Nora. "Color, Versatilidad, y Figuración." *Bazaar en Español,* January
1982, pp. 9–15.

Hunter, Sam. "Post Modern Painting." *Portfolio,* January/February 1982,
pp. 46–53.

Peters, Lisa. "David Salle." *Print Collector's Newsletter,* January/February 1982,
p. 182. (Illus.: *Until Photographs Could Be Taken from Earth Satellites,* b&w.)

Ratcliff, Carter. "David Salle." *Interview,* February 1982, pp. 64–66. (Illus.:
Cut Out the Beggar, c.)

———. "An Attack on Painting." *Saturday Review,* January 1982,
pp. 50–51.

de Coppet, Laura. "Leo Castelli." *Interview,* February 1982, pp. 60–62.

Staff. "David Salle, New York 1981." *Domus,* February 1982, p. 74.

Bangert, Albrecht. "Neue Kunst oder nur eine Neue Masche?" *Ambiente,*
February 1982.

Kontova, Helena. "From Performance to Painting." *Flash Art,* February/March
1982, p. 61.

Russell, John. "Art: David Salle." *The New York Times,* March 19, 1982,
p. C24.

Schjeldahl, Peter. "David Salle's Objects of Disaffection." *The Village Voice,* March 23, 1982, p. 83.

Smith, Roberta. "Mass Production." *The Village Voice,* March 23, 1982.

Larson, Kay. "David Salle." *New York Magazine,* March 29, 1982.

Pincus-Witten, Robert. "Gary Stephan: The Brief Against Matisse." *Arts Magazine,* March 1982, p. 83.

Plagens, Peter. "Issues and Commentary: Mixed Doubles." *Art in America,* March 1982, pp. 9–15.

Winter, Simon Vaughan. "Rubbing Our Noses in It." *The Art Magazine,* Winter 1982, pp. 2–5.

Fox, Catherine. "The Art of Equivocation." *The Atlanta Journal and Constitution,* April 10, 1982, p. 43.

Moufarrege, Nicholas. "The Eye of the Beholder." *New York Native,* April 12, 1982, pp. 32–33.

Haden-Guest, Anthony. "The New Queen of the Art Scene." *New York Magazine,* April 19, 1982, pp. 24–30.

Caroli, Flavio. "Magico Primario." *Interarte 23,* April 1982, pp. 5–27.

Pincus-Witten, Robert. "David Salle: Holiday Glassware." *Arts Magazine,* April 1982, pp. 58–60.

Agnese, Maria Luisa, and Carbonne, Fabrizio. "Ve lo do io Artista." *Panorama,* May 22, 1982, pp. 138–145.

Glueck, Grace. "Exhibits Focus on the Figure: Twenty Years at The Whitney Museum and Agitated Figures." *The New York Times,* May 30, 1982, sec. 2, p. 27.

Diehl, Carol. "Galleries: As Time Goes By." *Art and Auction,* May 1982, pp. 30–37.

Brewster, Todd. "Boone Means Business." *Life,* May 1982, pp. 30–37.

Reed, Susan. "The Meteoric Rise of Mary Boone." *Saturday Review,* May 1982, pp. 36–42.

Kosuth, Joseph. "Portraits . . . Necrophilia Mon Amour." *Artforum,* May 1982, pp. 59–65.

deAk, Edit, and Cortez, Diego. "Baby Talk." *Flash Art,* May 1982, pp. 34–38.

Nilson, Lisbeth. "The Sorceress of Soho." *Metropolitan Home,* June 1982, pp. 47–52.

Salle, David. "(Cover Illustration, C)." *The Paris Review,* Spring 1982.

Stevens, Mark. "The Revival of Realism." *Newsweek,* June 7, 1982, pp. 64–70.

Tomkins, Calvin. "The Art World." *The New Yorker,* June 7, 1982, pp. 120–125.

Smith, Roberta. "Group Flex." *The Village Voice,* June 22, 1982, p. 106.

Schjeldahl, Peter. "South of the Border." *The Village Voice*, June 29, 1982, p. 51.

Paley, Maggie. "Mary Boone: A Confident Vision." *Savvy*, June 1982, pp. 62–67.

Leibmann, Lisa. "David Salle." *Artforum*, Summer 1982, pp. 89–90.

Tucker, Marcia. "An Iconography of Recent Figurative Painting." *Artforum*, Summer 1982, pp. 70–75.

McGuigan, Cathleen. "Julian Schnabel." *Art News*, Summer 1982, pp. 88–94.

Secrest, Meryle. "Leo Castelli: Dealing in Myth." *Art News*, Summer 1982, pp. 66–72.

Kuspit, Donald. "David Salle at Mary Boone and Castelli." *Art in America*, Summer 1982, p. 142.

Oliva, Achille Bonito. "Avant Garde and Trans-Avantgarde." *Interarte 24*, June 1982, pp. 6–32.

Parker, William. "Expressionism Is Back in Fashion." *The Times* (London), July 6, 1982.

Feaver, William. "A Bad Case of Hype." *Observer Review/Arts*, July 11, 1982, p. 30.

Russell, John. "In the Arts: Critics' Choices." *The New York Times*, July 11, 1982, sec. 2, p. 1.

Doherty, M. Stephen. "Hype Returns to the Art World." *American Artist*, July 1982, p. 6.

Kalil, Susie. "Americans: The Collage." *The Houston Post*, July 18, 1982, p. 16AA.

Schjeldahl, Peter. "King Curator." *The Village Voice*, July 20, 1982, p. 73.

Unger, Craig. "Attitude." *New York Magazine*, July 26, 1982, p. 73.

Goldberg, Roselee. "Post-TV Art." *Portfolio*, July/August 1982, pp. 76–79.

Wallace, Joan, and Donahue, Geralyn. "You Wish You Were Closer to You." *ZG Magazine*, No. 7.

Caroli, Flavio. "I Mondiali del Giovanni." *Arte*, August 1982, pp. 35–42. (Illus.: *Proust or Canada*, c.)

Lowe, Ron. "FWAM Exhibit Jolts Viewers into the 80's." *The Fort Worth Star Telegram*, September 12, 1982, p. E1. (Illus.: *Unexpectedly I Miss Cousin Jasper*, p. E1, c.)

Marvel, Bill. "The Art of the 80's: A Return to Reality." *The Dallas Times Herald*, September 15, 1982, p. F1.

Kunter, Janet. "Voice for the 1980's Cutting Edge." *Dallas Morning News*, September 15, 1982.

Kalil, Susie. "American Collage Since 1950." *Artweek*, September, 18, 1982, pp. 1–26.

Price, Katherine. "Arte USA." *Nouvi Argomenti*, September 1982, pp. 32–40. (Illus.: *The Worst and Most General*, c.)

Bangert, Albrecht. "Neue Kunst oder eine Neue Masche?" *Ambiente*, September 1982, pp. 15–16.

deAk, Edit. "Stalling Art." *Artforum*, September 1982, pp. 71–75. (Illus.: *The Happy Writers*, b&w.)

Yoskowitz, Robert. "David Salle at Mary Boone." *Arts Magazine*, September 1982, p. 34.

Robins, Corrine. "Ten Months of Rush-Hour Figuration." *Arts Magazine*, September 1982, pp. 100–103. (Illus.: *The Name Painting*, b&w.)

Gendel, Milton. "Report from Venice." *Art in America*, September 1982, pp. 33–39.

Reichard, Steven. "David Salle." *In Performance*, September 1982, p. 3. (Illus.: *Seeing Sight*, cover, c.)

Haime, Nora. "25 Años de Exito: Leo Castelli." *Bazaar en Español*, September 1982, pp. 78–106. (Illus.: *Untitled*, pp. 78–79, c).

Anderson, Alexandra. "Critic's Choice." *Portfolio*, September 1982, p. 57.

Marzorati, Gerald. "Documenta 7." *Portfolio*, September 1982, pp. 92–95.

Ratcliff, Carter. "David Salle's Aquatints." *Print Collector's Newsletter*, September/October 1982, pp. 123–126.

———. "A Season in New York." *Art International*, September/October 1982, pp. 54–60. (Illus.: *Splinter Man*, p. 54, b&w.)

Staff. "Der Zeitgeist weht durch den Palazzo." *Der Spiegel*, October 11, 1982, pp. 241–244. (Illus.: *Zeitgeist Painting #1*, c.)

Schjeldahl, Peter. "Clemente to Marden to Kiefer." *The Village Voice*, October 12, 1982, p. 83.

Grosskopf, Annegret. "Bomben-Stimmung '82." *Stern*, October 14, 1982, pp. 187–203. (Illus.: *Zeitgeist Painting #2*, c.)

Smith, Roberta. "Everyman's Land." *The Village Voice*, October 26, 1982, p. 98.

Larson, Kay. "L'Art." *Vogue Paris*, October 1982, pp. 342–348.

Greenspan, Stuart. "Americans Abroad." *Art and Auction*, October 1982, pp. 36–43.

Silverthorne, Jeanne. "The Pressure to Paint." *Artforum*, October 1982, pp. 67–68.

Kirshner, Judith Russi. "74th American Exhibition." *Artforum*, October 1982, pp. 74–75.

Moufarrege, Nicholas. "Lavender: On Homosexuality and Art." *Arts Magazine*, October 1982, pp. 78–87.

Frackman, Noel, and Kaufmann, Ruth. "Documenta 7: The Dialogue and a Few Asides." *Arts Magazine*, October 1982, pp. 91–97.

Ponti, Lisa. "Documenta 7." *Domus*, October 1982, pp. 67–74.

Wolf, Deborah. "Mary Boone." *Avenue*, October 1982, pp. 40–47. (Illus.: *The Wild One, The Blue Room*, c.)

Olosso, Anna. "New York—Tur + Retur." *Expressen*, November 27, 1982, p. 5.

Colacello, Bob. "Out." *Interview*, November 1982, pp. 93–94.

Greenspan, Stuart. "Plus C'est la Même Chose." *Art and Auction*, November 1982, pp. 58–62.

Kramer, Hilton. "Signs of Passion: The New Expressionism." *The New Criterion*, November 1982, pp. 40–45.

Joachimides, Christos. "Zeitgeist." *Flash Art*, November 1982, pp. 26–31.

Groot, Paul. "David Salle." *Flash Art*, November 1982, pp. 69–70.

Ponti, Lisa. "Mary Boone and the Past and the Present and the Future." *Domus*, November 1982, pp. 72–73.

Torri, Maria Grazia. "L'Avventura di Bonaventura." *Juliet*, November 1982/ January 1983, pp. 8–9.

Wingenerte, Ed. "David Salle der Werkelijkheid vertuoos samen." *De Telegraf*, December 4, 1982, p. T23.

Russell, John. "A Big Berlin Show That Misses the Mark." *The New York Times*, December 5, 1982, p. C33.

Staff. "Notities." *Buitenlust*, December 9, 1982.

Van Houts, Catherine, and Klaster, Jan Bart. "Als Kunstenaar be je alleen." *Buitenlust*, December 11, 1982.

Schenke, Menno. "Tentoonstelling van schilder David Salle in Amsterdam." *Algmeen Dagblad*, December 17, 1982, p. 19.

Smith, Roberta. "Didacticism, Material, Immaterial." *The Village Voice*, December 21, 1982, p. 113.

Geldzahler, Henry. "Determining Aesthetic Values." *Interview*, December 1982, pp. 29–31.

Ratcliff, Carter. "Expressionism Today: An Artist's Symposium." *Art in America*, December 1982, pp. 58–75.

Clarke, John. "Up Against the Wall, Transavanguardia." *Arts Magazine*, December 1982, pp. 76–81.

Reynolds, Anthony. "Zeitgeist." *Art Monthly*, December 1982, pp. 11–12.

Leccese, Pasquale. "Zeitgeist." *Domus*, December 1982, pp. 70–74.

Staff. "Galleries: David Salle." *Mode*, December 1982.

Staff. "David Salle." *Justitia*, December 1982.

Glueck, Grace. "Artists Who Scavenge from the Media." *The New York Times*, January 9, 1983, sec. 2, p. 29.

Brenson, Michael. "New York vs. Paris: Views of an Art Reporter." *The New York Times*, January 16, 1983, sec. 2, p. 1.

Nechvetal, Joseph. "Epic Images and Contemporary History." *Real Life*, Winter 1983, pp. 22–26. (Illus.: *It Goes Without Saying That the Flour Sack Strikes the Rat Dead*, b&w.)

Strenko, Michael. "What's an Artist to Do? A Short History of Postmodernism and Photography." *Afterimage*, January 1983, pp. 4–5.

Blau, Douglas. "Kim MacConnel: David Salle." *Arts Magazine*, January 1983, pp. 62–63.

Saatchi, Doris. "Zeitgeist: Wurst at Its Best." *Art Monthly*, January 1983, pp. 12–15.

Aletrino, David. "David Salle." *Tableau*, January 1983, p. 266.

Robbins, D. A. "The 'Meaning' of 'New'—the '70s/'80s Axis: An Interview with Diego Cortez." *Arts Magazine*, January 1983, pp. 116–121.

Owens, Craig. "Honor, Power and Love of Women." *Art in America*, January 1983, pp. 7–13.

Ratcliff, Carter. "The Short Life of the Sincere Stroke." *Art in America*, January 1983, pp. 73–137.

Crary, Jonathan. "The Expressionist Image at Janis." *Art in America*, January 1983, pp. 119–120.

Groot, Paul. "Further Opinions on Documenta 7." *Flash Art*, January 1983, pp. 24–25.

Smith, Roberta. "Appropriation uber alles." *The Village Voice*, January 11, 1983, p. 73.

Levin, Kim. "Art: David Salle." *The Village Voice*, February 16, 1983, centerfold.

Raynor, Vivien. "Soho: Enough Space for Extremes of Style." *The New York Times*, February 18, 1983, p. C24.

Greenspan, Stuart. "Leo Castelli." *Art and Auction*, February 1983, pp. 62–64.

———. "Donald Marron." *Art and Auction*, February 1983, pp. 65–67.

———. "Contemporary Art." *Art and Auction*, February 1983, p. 69.

Pincus-Witten, Robert. "Entries: Vaulting Ambition." *Arts Magazine*, February 1983, pp. 70–75.

Morgan, Stuart. "David Salle at Anthony D'Offay." *Artscribe*, February 1983.

Smith, Roberta. "Making Impressions." *The Village Voice*, March 1, 1983, p. 79.

King, Mary. "Salle Paintings." *St. Louis Post-Dispatch*, March 9, 1983, p. D4.

Farber, Julea. "Rotterdam Museum Shows David Salle." *International Herald Tribune*, March 12, 1983, p. 11.

Moss, Jacqueline. "David Salle and Roberta Smith on Art at Whitney Museum."

Hughes, Robert. "Three from the Image Machine." *Time*, March 14, 1983, pp. 83–84.

Richard, Paul. "Avant-Garde Airs." *The Washington Post*, March 15, 1983, p. C1.

Allen, Jane Adams. "American Art Takes Cynical Course at The Hirshhorn." *The Washington Times Magazine*, March 15, 1983, pp. E4–5.

Glueck, Grace. "Art: Big American Figure Drawings." *The New York Times*, March 18, 1983, p. C23.

Rubin, Michael. "Salle's Paintings Show at Greenberg Gallery." *St. Louis Globe Democrat*, March 19–20, 1983, p. F11.

Moss, Jacqueline. "So Where Are the Women at the Whitney?" *The Greenwich Times*, March 27, 1983, p. D1.

Glueck, Grace. "Two Biennials: One Looking East and the Other West." *The New York Times*, March 27, 1983, sec. 2, p. 35.

Schjeldahl, Peter. "Falling in Style." *Vanity Fair*, March 1983, p. 115.

Roberts, John. "An Interview with David Salle." *Art Monthly*, March 1983, pp. 3–7.

Dimitrijevic, Nena. "David Salle." *Flash Art*, March 1983, p. 66.

Glueck, Grace. "One Man's Biennial Assembles 102 Artists." *The New York Times*, April 15, 1983, p. C24.

Ashbery, John. "Biennials Bloom in the Spring." *Newsweek*, April 18, 1983, pp. 93–94.

Levin, Kim. "Double Takes." *The Village Voice*, April 26, 1983, p. 91.

Smith, Roberta. "Talking Consensus." *The Village Voice*, April 26, 1983, p. 91.

Wohlfert-Wihlborg, Lee. "Europe's Exuberant New Wave Artists." *Town and Country*, April 1983, pp. 180–194.

Schjeldahl, Peter. "Up Against the Wall." *Vanity Fair*, April 1983, p. 93.

Moufarrege, Nicholas. "Intoxication: April 9 1983." *Arts Magazine*, April 1983, pp. 70–76. (Illus.: *We'll Shake the Bag*, b&w.)

Brenson, Michael. "Artists Grapple with New Realities." *The New York Times*, May 15, 1983, sec. 2, p. 1.

Staff. "Self Portraits." *New York Magazine*, May 23, 1983, pp. 30–35.

Nayhausse, Sabine Grafin. "Neue Kunst satt Tapetenwechsel." *Ambiente*, May 1983, pp. 138–145.

Vidali, Roberto. "L'Imbarazzante Clima Estetico di David Salle." *Juliet*, May 1983, pp. 24–25.

Fawcett, Anthony, and Withers, Jane. "Commercial Art." *The Face*, May 1983, pp. 75–77. (Illus.: *Before No Walk*, b&w.)

Moufarrege, Nicholas. "David Salle." *Flash Art*, May 1983, p. 60.

Honnef, Klaus. "Tagebuch einer Dienstreise." *Kunstforum*, May 1983, pp. 32–123.

Liebmann, Lisa. "David Salle." *Artforum*, Summer 1983, p. 74. (Illus.: *Zeitgeist Painting #1, Zeitgeist Painting #4*, b&w.)

Cameron, Dan. "Biennial Cycle." *Arts Magazine*, June 1983, pp. 64–66. (Illus.: *Poverty Is No Disgrace*, p. 66, c.)

Staff. "Zeitgeist." *Art Vivant*, July 1983, pp. 19–78.

Lovelace, Carey. "Painting for Dollars." *Harper's Magazine*, July 1983, pp. 66–70. (Illus.: *Ugly Deaf Face*, b&w.)

Piot, Christine. "Manet et Amérique." *Art Press*, July/August 1983, pp. 20–22.

Walker, John. "David Salle's Exemplary Perversity." *Tension Magazine*, July/
August 1983, pp. 14–17. (Illus.: *The Wild Bunch*, b&w; *Before No Walk*,
b&w; *To Count Steps With*, b&w.)

Smith, Roberta. "Comics Stripped." *The Village Voice*, August 23, 1983,
p. 94.

Wintour, Anna. "Painting the Town." *New York Magazine*, August 29, 1983,
p. 53. (Illus.: *The Life of a Shrug* [detail], c.)

Schwartz, Eugene. "Guerilla Tactics for Collectors in Today's Emerging Art
Market." *Bottom Line*, September 30, 1983, pp. 9–10.

Hegewisch, Katharina. "Eine besondere Art der Erotik, David Salle in
München und Hamburg." *Frankfurter Allgemeine Zeitung*, October 18, 1983.

Glozer, Laszlo. "Dialog mit den Ahnen, Zwei Ausstellungen in der Münchner
Maximillianstrasse." *Suddeutsche Zeitung*, October 26, 1983.

Hughes, Robert. "There's No Geist like Zeitgeist." *The New York Review of
Books*, October 27, 1983, p. 63.

Kipphoff, Petra. "Hamburg: 'David Salle.' " *Die Zeit*, October 28, 1983.

Zimmer, William. " 'Before' and 'After' Look from the Coast." *The New York
Times*, October 30, 1983, sec. 22, p. 20.

Staff. "Schellman & Kluser stellt Picabia aus." *Münchner Abendzeitung*,
October 1983.

Forte, Gabriella. "A Colpi di Pennello: David Salle Sabotaggio d'Artista."
L'Uomo Vogue, October 1983, pp. 342–343.

Larson, Kay. "How Should Artists Be Educated?" *Art News*, November 1983,
pp. 85–91. (Illus.: *We'll Shake the Bag*, p. 89, c.)

Staff. "Ein Potpourri der Stile: Francis Picabia and David Salle." *Münchner
Theaterzeitung*, November 1983.

Cohen, Ronny. "The New Graphic Sensibility Transcends Media." *Print
Collector's Newsletter*, November/December 1983, pp. 157–159.

Schultz, Sabine. "Back to the USA." *Die Kunst*, December 1983, pp. 827–
834. (Illus.: *Past*, c.)

Staff. "Francis Picabia and David Salle." *Flash Art*, January 1984, p. 31. (Illus.:
Melancholy, b&w.)

Larson, Kay. "Art: Antidotes to Irony." *New York Magazine*, February 27,
1984, pp. 58–59.

Geldzahler, Henry. "Guest Speaker: On Breaking the Rules." *Architectural
Digest*, February 1984, pp. 26–32. (Illus.: *Zeitgeist Painting #2*, c.)

Staff. "New Painting Phenomenon." *Brutus*, February 1984, pp. 26–68. (Illus.:
To Count Steps With, p. 53, c.)

Pincus-Witten, Robert. "I-Know-That-You-Know-That-I-Know." *Arts
Magazine*, February 1984, pp. 126–129. (Illus.: *Tennyson*, b&w;
B.A.M.F.V., b&w.)

Ratcliff, Carter. "The Inscrutable Jasper Johns." *Vanity Fair*, February 1984,
pp. 61–65.

Brenson, Michael. "Art: Variety of Forms for David Salle Imagery." *The New York Times*, March 23, 1984, p. C20. (Illus.: *B.A.M.F.V.*, b&w.)

Schjeldahl, Peter. "Spain: The Structure of Ritual." *Vanity Fair*, March 1984, pp. 58–67.

Pincus-Witten, Robert. "Entries: Propaedeutica." *Arts Magazine*, March 1984, pp. 94–96.

Cameron, Dan. "Against Collaboration." *Arts Magazine*, March 1984, pp. 83–87. (Illus.: *Jump*, b&w.)

Smith, Roberta. "Quality Is the Best Revenge." *The Village Voice*, April 3, 1984, p. 79.

Larson, Kay. "The Low Road to Soho." *New York Magazine*, April 9, 1984, pp. 68–69. (Illus.: *What Is the Reason for Your Visit to Germany*, c.)

Schwartz, Sanford. "David Salle: The Art World." *The New Yorker*, April 30, 1984, pp. 104–111.

Nemeczek, Alfred. "Magnet New York." *Art*, May 1984, p. 35. (Illus.: *Zeitgeist Painting #2*, c.)

Ponti, Lisa. "Artist's Loft One: David Salle." *Domus*, June 1984, pp. 40–41. (Illus.: *King Kong*, c.)

Raynor, Vivien. "Art: 3 Friends Who Share Attitudes and a Show." *The New York Times*, July 20, 1984, p. C20.

Glueck, Grace. "A Neo-Expressionist Survey That's Worth a Journey." *The New York Times*, July 22, 1984, sec. 2, p. 25.

Solway, Diane. "Entertainment in View." *M*, July 1984, pp. 155–157.

Marzorati, Gerald. "The Artful Dodger." *Artnews*, Summer 1984, pp. 47–55. (Illus.: *His Brain*, p. 49, c; *Brother Animal*, p. 50, c; *Tennyson*, p. 51, c; *The Cruelty of the Father*, p. 51, c; *Burning Bush*, p. 52, c; *How Close the Ass of a Horse Was to Actual Glue and Dog Food*, p. 54, b&w.)

Kohn, Michael. "David Salle." *Flash Art*, Summer 1984, p. 68. (Illus.: *His Brain*, p. 68, b&w.)

Bourdon, David. "Uproar: Clutter and Clatter at the Modern." *Vogue*, August 1984, p. 72.

Levin, Kim. "From the Familiar to the Sublime." *The Village Voice*, September 11, 1984, p. 77.

Robinson, John. "Francesco Clemente/Bryan Hunt/David Salle." *Arts Magazine*, September 1984, p. 34.

Schjeldahl, Peter. "The Real Salle." *Art in America*, September 1984, pp. 180–187. (Illus.: *What Is the Reason for Your Visit to Germany*, pp. 180–181, c; *Brother Animal*, p. 182, b&w; *Portrait of Michael Hurson*, p. 182, b&w; *His Brain*, p. 183, c; *The Face in the Column*, p. 184, b&w; *B.A.M.F.V.*, p.185, c; *Tennyson*, p. 186, c; *Midday*, p.187, c.)

Viladas, Pilar. "Free Association: Salle Loft, New York." *Progressive Architecture*, September 1984, pp. 120–123.

Millet, Catherine. "L'Ingratitude de l'Art." *Art Press*, October 1984, pp. 4–12. (Illus.: *The Face in the Column*, p. 7, b&w; *What Is the Reason for Your Visit to Germany*, pp. 10–11, b&w.)

Brenson, Michael. "Art: Julian Schnabel the Carnival Man." *The New York Times*, November 9, 1984, p. C24.

———. "Human Figure Is Back in Unlikely Guises." *The New York Times*, January 13, 1985, sec. 2, p. 1.

Filler, Martin. "Tribeca Textures." *House & Garden*, February 1985, pp. 128–135. (Illus.: *Brother Animal*, p. 130, c.)

Brooks, Rosetta. "From the Night of Consumerism to the Dawn of Simulation." *Artforum*, February 1985, pp. 76–81. (Illus.: *What Is the Reason for Your Visit to Germany*, p. 77, c.)

Pincus-Witten, Robert. "Entries: Analytical Pubism." *Arts Magazine*, February 1985, p. 85. (Illus.: *What Is the Reason for Your Visit to Germany*, p. 85, b&w.)

Richard, Nelly. "Notes Towards a (Critical) Re-evaluation of the Critique of the Avant-Garde." *Art and Text*, Summer 1984 / 1985, pp. 15–19. (Illus.: *King Kong*, p. 19, b&w.)

McGuigan, Cathleen. "New Art, New Money: The Marketing of an American Artist." *The New York Times Magazine*, February 10, 1985, p. 20. (Illus.: *Miner*, p. 22, c.)

Millet, Catherine. "La Peinture que le Regard Disperse." *Art Press*, February 1985, pp. 18–21. (Illus.: *Midday*, p. 18, b&w; *A Minute*, p. 19, b&w; *The Blood Traffic*, p. 20, b&w; *His Brain*, p. 21, b&w.)

Russell, John. "Whitney Presents Its Biennial Exhibition." *The New York Times*, March 22, 1985, p. C23.

Staff. "The Top 100 American Collectors." *Art & Antiques*, March 1985, p. 45.

Tazy, Nadia. "Eloge de l'Ambiguïté." *L'Autre Journal*, March 1985, pp. 51–52. (Illus.: *Brother Animal*, p. 51, c; *His Brain*, p. 51, c.)

Venant, Elizabeth. "Rebel Expressions." *Los Angeles Times Calendar*, April 28, 1985, pp. 4–7. (Illus.: *Pauper*, p. 6, b&w.)

Smith, Roberta. "Endless Meaning at the Hirshhorn." *Artforum*, April 1985, pp. 81–85.

Brenson, Michael. "Art: David Salle Show at Mary Boone Gallery." *The New York Times*, May 3, 1985, p. C25. (Illus.: *Miner*, p. C25, b&w.)

Salle, David. "Gemini G.E.L.: Art and Collaboration." *Artforum*, May 1985, p. 3.

Staniszewski, Mary Anne. "Corporate Culture/Gallery Guide." *Manhattan, Inc.*, May 1985, pp. 136–137. (Illus.: *Miner*, p. 137, c.)

Larson, Kay. "The Daring of David Salle." *New York Magazine*, May 20, 1985, p. 98. (Illus.: *Miner*, p. 98, c.)

McGill, Douglas. "Artist's Style Wins High Praise—and Rejection." *The New York Times*, May 16, 1985, p. C23.

Levin, Kim. "Artwalk—David Salle." *The Village Voice*, May 28, 1985, p. 100. (Illus.: *Muscular Paper*, p. 100, b&w.)

Honnef, Klaus. "Nouvelle Biennale de Paris." *Kunstforum*, May/June 1985, pp. 216–232. (Illus.: *His Brain*, p. 230, c; *Portrait of Asher Edelman*, p. 230, c.)

Hughes, Robert. "Careerism and Hype Amidst the Image Haze." *Time*, June 17, 1985, pp. 78–83. (Illus.: *Miner*, p. 79, c.)

Larson, Kay. "Boomtown Hype—and Real Quality." *New York Magazine*, June 17, 1985, pp. 46–47.

Perrone, Jeff. "The Salon of 1985." *Arts Magazine*, Summer 1985, pp. 70–73. (Illus.: *The Disappearance of the Booming Voice*, p. 72, b&w.)

Marzorati, Gerald. "Picture Puzzles: The Whitney Biennial." *Art News*, Summer 1985, pp. 74–78. (Illus.: *B.A.M.F.V.*, p. 75, c.)

Millet, Catherine. "David Salle." *Flash Art*, Summer 1985, pp. 30–34. (Illus.: *Din*, p. 30, c; *Making the Bed*, p. 31, c; *A Minute*, p. 32, c; *Muscular Paper*, p. 33, c; *Poverty Is No Disgrace*, p. 33, c.)

Pincus-Witten, Robert. "Interview with David Salle." *Flash Art*, Summer 1985, pp. 35–36. (Illus.: *My Head*, p. 35, c.)

Kohn, Michael. "Whitney Biennial." *Flash Art*, Summer 1985, p. 54.

Russell, John. "Modern Art Museums: The Surprise Is Gone." *The New York Times*, August 4, 1985, sec. 2, p. 1.

Stein, Margery. "A Question of Taste." *Smart Living*, September 1985, pp. 19–22. (Illus.: *The Bigger Credenza*, p. 20, b&w.)

Madoff, Steven Henry. "What Is Postmodern about Painting: The Scandinavia Lectures." *Arts Magazine*, September 1985, pp. 116–121. (Illus.: *A Collapsing Sheet*, p. 118, c.)

Grimes, Nancy. "New York Reviews, David Salle." *Art News*, September 1985, p. 133. (Illus.: *Miner*, p. 133, b&w.)

Rose, Barbara. "Art in Discoland." *Vogue*, September 1985, pp. 668–672, 747. (Illus.: *Shower of Courage*, p. 670, c.)

Liebmann, Lisa. "Wham! Slam! Thank You BAM." *Vogue*, October 1985, p. 120.

Clarke, John R. "Circuses and Bread: Achille Bonito Oliva's Nouve Trame Dell'Arte at Genazzano." *Arts Magazine*, October 1985, pp. 34–39.

Madoff, Steven Henry. "What Is Postmodern about Painting: The Scandinavia Lectures, II." *Arts Magazine*, October 1985, pp. 59–64.

Ratcliff, Carter. "Dramatis Personae, Part II: The Scheherazade Tactic." *Art in America*, October 1985, pp. 9–13.

Marsh, Georgia. "David Salle." *Bomb*, Fall 1985, pp. 20–25. (Illus.: *The Disappearance of the Booming Voice*, p. 21, b&w; *Pauper*, p. 23, b&w; *The Bigger Credenza*, p. 25, b&w.)

Kuspit, Donald. "David Salle, Mary Boone Gallery." *Artforum*, November 1985, pp. 103–104. (Illus.: *Muscular Paper*, p. 103, b&w.)

McCormick, Carlo. "Poptometry." *Artforum*, November 1985, pp. 87–91.

Cameron, Dan. "The Salle Academy." *Arts Magazine*, November 1985, pp. 74–77. (Illus.: *Géricault's Arm*, p. 74, c; *Sleeping in the Corners*, p. 74, c; *Fooling with Your Hair*, p. 75, c; *Words Go Crying*, p. 75, c.)

Pincus-Witten, Robert. "An Interview with David Salle." *Arts Magazine*, November 1985, pp. 78–81. (Illus.: *The Farewell Painting*, cover and p. 78, c; *Salt Banners*, p. 79, c; *Low Cost Color Numbers*, p. 80, b&w.)

Olive, Kristan. "David Salle's Deconstructive Strategy." *Arts Magazine*, November 1985, pp. 82–85. (Illus.: *Portrait of Asher Edelman*, p. 82, b&w; *A Collapsing Sheet*, p. 83, b&w; *What Is the Reason for Your Visit to Germany*, p. 84, b&w; *His Brain*, p. 85, b&w.)

Feinstein, Roni. "David Salle's Art in 1985: Dead or Alive?" *Arts Magazine*, November 1985, pp. 86–88. (Illus.: *Making the Bed*, p. 86, b&w; *The Bigger Credenza*, p. 86, b&w; *Shower of Courage*, p. 87, b&w; *My Head*, p. 87, b&w.)

Staniszewski, Mary Anne. "Corporate Culture." *Manhattan, Inc.*, December 1985, p. 146. (Illus.: *Delicately Emblematic Subdivision*, p. 146, c; *The Farewell Painting*, p. 146, c.)

Bromberg, Craig. "The Crest of the Wave." *Vanity Fair*, December 1985, pp. 126–128.

Rockwell, John. " 'Birth of a Poet,' Avant-Garde." *The New York Times*, December 5, 1985, p. C17.

Hughes, Robert. "Tracing the Underground Stream." *Time*, December 23, 1985, pp. 74–75.

Cohen, Ronny. "Cutting a New Figure." *Town and Country*, January 1986, pp. 163–164. (Illus.: *Untitled*, p. 164, c.)

Brenson, Michael. "Is Neo-Expressionism an Idea Whose Time Has Passed?" *The New York Times*, January 5, 1986, sec. 2, p. 1. (Illus.: *B.A.M.F.V.*, p. 12, b&w.)

Wetzsteon, Ross. "Culture Czar." *The Village Voice*, January 15, 1986, pp. 21–26.

Kaufman, David. "The Death of the Avant-Garde." *SAW*, January 15, 1986, p. 19B.

Lawson, Thomas. "Toward Another Laocoon or, the Snake Pit." *Artforum*, March 1986, pp. 97–106. (Illus.: *Miner*, p. 104, c.)

Schwartz, Sanford. "The Saatchi Collection, or a Generation Comes into Focus." *The New Criterion*, March 1986, pp. 22–37.

Kass, Ray. "Current Milestones." *Dialogue*, March/April 1986, pp. 17–19.

Staniszewski, Mary Anne. "Gallery Guide." *Manhattan, Inc.*, April 1986, p. 164. (Illus.: *Footmen*, p. 164, c.)

De Smecchia, Muni. "Gli Artisti nel Loro Studio: David Salle." *Vogue Italia,* February 1986, pp. 296–301, 324. (Illus.: *Coral Made,* pp. 298–299, c.)

Raynor, Vivien. "David Salle." *The New York Times,* April 11, 1986, p. C30.

Tuchman, Phyllis. "David Salle, Emerging as a Young Master." *New York Newsday,* April 20, 1986, part II, p. 11. (Illus.: *Dusting Powders,* p. 11, b&w.)

Indiana, Gary. "Art: David Salle." *The Village Voice,* April 29, 1986, p. 74.

Kuspit, Donald. "David Salle's Aesthetic of Discontent." *C Magazine,* Spring 1986, pp. 23–27. (Illus.: *Muscular Paper,* p. 23, b&w; *Poverty Is No Disgrace,* pp. 24–25, b&w; *The Disappearance of the Booming Voice,* p. 27, b&w.)

Brenson, Michael. "Romanticism or Cynicism? Only Salle Knows." *The New York Times,* April 27, 1986, sec. 2, p. 31. (Illus.: *Footmen,* p. 31, b&w.)

Indiana, Gary. "Apotheosis of the Non-moment." *The Village Voice,* May 6, 1986, p. 91. (Illus.: *Pastel,* p. 91, b&w.)

Rubinstein, Meyer Raphael, and Wiener, Daniel. "David Salle." *Arts Magazine,* Summer 1986, p. 105. (Illus.: *The Raffael,* p. 105, b&w.)

Parks, Addison. "David Salle." *Arts Magazine,* Summer 1986, p. 116.

Dimitrijevic, Nena. "Alice in Culturescapes." *Flash Art,* Summer 1986, pp. 50–54. (Illus.: *Schoolroom,* p. 50, c.)

Duret-Robert, François. "Les Peintres d'Aujourd'hui dont on Parlera Demain." *Connaissance des Arts,* July/August 1986, pp. 42–53. (Illus.: *Dusting Powders,* p. 47, c.)

Politi, Giancarlo. "David Salle." *Flash Art Edition Française,* Summer 1986, pp. 12–17. (Illus.: *Muscular Paper,* p. 12, c; *A Minute,* p. 13, c; *Making the Bed,* p. 13, c; *The Cold Child* (for George Trow), p. 14, c; *Poverty Is No Disgrace,* p. 14, b&w; *My Head,* p. 15, c; *His Brain,* p. 16, b&w; *Din,* p. 17, c.)

Brenson, Michael. "Art: Modern Masters, Ancient Treasures, and New Questions." *The New York Times,* September 7, 1986, sec. 2, p. 43.

Newhall, Edith. "Art: Fall Preview." *New York Magazine,* September 1986, pp. 64–78.

Pincus-Witten, Robert. "David Salle: Sightatations (From the Theater of the Deaf to the Géricault Paintings)." *Arts Magazine,* October 1986, pp. 40–44. (Illus.: *Sterotropic,* p. 40, b&w; *Colony,* p. 43, c.)

Staff. "Album: David Salle." *Arts Magazine,* October 1986, pp. 114–115. (Illus.: *Pastel,* p. 114, b&w; *We'll Shake the Bag,* p. 114, b&w; *View the Author Through Long Telescopes,* p. 115, b&w; *Shower of Courage,* p. 115, b&w.)

Johnston, Jill. "Dance: The Punk Princess and the Postmodern Prince." *Art in America,* October 1986, pp. 23–25.

Kohn, Michael. "David Salle." *Flash Art,* October/November 1986, p. 72. (Illus.: *The Train,* p. 72, b&w.)

Heartney, Elinor. "New Editions: David Salle." *Art News*, October 1986, p. 101. (Illus.: *Grandiose Synonym for Church*, p. 100, c.)

Staff. "An Artist for the Eighties." *The Pennsylvania Gazette*, October 1986, pp. 43–45. (Illus.: *King Kong*, p. 43, c; *Brother Animal*, p. 44, c; *Black Bra*, p. 44, c; *Archer's House*, p. 45, c; *Tennyson*, p. 45, c; *His Brain*, p. 45, c.)

Silverthorne, Jeanne. "David Salle." *Artforum*, November 1986, p. 133. (Illus.: *Dusting Powders*, p. 133, b&w.)

Kramer, Hilton. "The Salle Phenomenon." *Art and Antiques*, December 1986, pp. 97–99.

Fernandes, Joyce. "Exposing a Phallocentric Discourse." *The New Art Examiner*, December 1986, pp. 32–34. (Illus.: *His Brain*, p. 32, b&w; *Timbre*, p. 33, b&w.)

Staff. "Artsmart." *Harper's Bazaar*, January 1987, pp. 164–166. (Illus.: *Pastel*, p. 164, c.)

Taylor, Paul. "How David Salle Mixes High Art and Trash." *The New York Times Magazine*, January 11, 1987, pp. 26–28, 39. (Illus.: *Landscape with Two Nudes and Three Eyes*, p. 26, c; *We'll Shake the Bag*, p. 28, c; *Coral Made*, p. 28, c.)

Wallach, Amei. "David Salle, There's a Mystery in His Art." *New York Newsday*, January 16, 1987, part III, p. 1. (Illus.: *Footmen*, p. 23, b&w; *Lost Barn Process*, p. 23, b&w; *Shower of Courage*, p. 23, b&w.)

Smith, Roberta. "Art: David Salle's Works Shown at the Whitney." *The New York Times*, January 23, 1987, p. C20. (Illus.: *Tennyson*, p. C20, b&w.)

Liebmann, Lisa. "Harlequinade for an Empty Room: On David Salle." *Artforum*, February 1987, pp. 94–99. (Illus.: *The Life of a Shrug*, p. 94, c; *Leg*, p. 95, c; *Schoolroom*, p. 97, c; *Landscape with Two Nudes and Three Eyes*, p. 98, c; *Backdrop from The Birth of a Poet*, p. 98, c; *Cut Out the Beggar*, p. 98, c; Backdrop from *The Elizabethan Phrasing of the Late Albert Ayler*, p. 99, c.)

Levin, Kim. "The Salle Question." *The Village Voice*, February 3, 1987, p. 81. (Illus.: *Fooling with Your Hair*, p. 81, b&w; *Brother Animal*, p. 82, b&w; *Ugly Deaf Face*, p. 82, b&w; *Black Bra*, p. 82, b&w.)

Flam, Jack. "David Salle: Neither a Hoax nor a Genius." *The Wall Street Journal*, January 29, 1987, p. 26.

Staniszewski, Mary Anne. "Gallery Guide: Home Style." *Manhattan, Inc.*, February 1987, p. 141. (Illus.: *Brother Animal*, p. 141, c.)

Larson, Kay. "The Big Tease." *New York Magazine*, February 9, 1987, pp. 58–59. (Illus.: *Géricault's Arm*, p. 58, c.)

Hughes, Robert. "Random Bits from the Image Haze." *Time*, February 9, 1987, pp. 67–68. (Illus.: *Footmen*, p. 67, c.)

PETER SCHJELDAHL

Peter Schjeldahl was born in 1942 in Fargo, North Dakota, and attended Carleton College and The New School. Formerly an art critic for the Sunday *New York Times*, *The Village Voice* and *Vanity Fair*, he is currently a contributing editor to *Art in America*. In addition to his many articles in major art journals in the United States and abroad, he has contributed to several art books and exhibition catalogues and has published five books of poetry, including *Since 1964: New and Selected Poems*. He is a recipient of the 1980 Frank Jewett Mather Award for excellence in art criticism from the College Art Association. He has lived in New York City since 1964.

Other books in

ELIZABETH AVEDON EDITIONS

VINTAGE CONTEMPORARY ARTISTS SERIES

FRANCESCO CLEMENTE

interviewed by Rainer Crone
and Georgia Marsh

ERIC FISCHL

interviewed by Donald Kuspit

ROBERT RAUSCHENBERG

interviewed by Barbara Rose